Online Personal Brand
Skill Set, Aura, and Identity

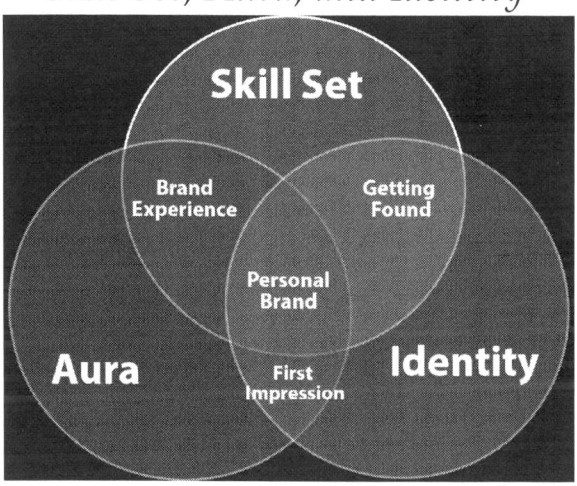

By Ryan Matthew Frischmann

Copyright © 2014 **Ryan M. Frischmann**
All rights reserved.

ISBN: **1500370983**
ISBN 13: **978-1500370985 (CreateSpace-Assigned)**

In this book, I take a logical step forward from my last book *A Skills-Based Approach to Developing a Career* by discussing the elements of an online personal brand: a skill set represents your functional value, an aura represents your emotional value, and an identity represents your connectedness.

The idea of a personal brand was first stated by Tom Peters in a *Fast Company* article back in 1997. Since this article, there have been many books, articles, and blogs written on the subject and now it is the buzz. Most of the interpretations are rooted in marketing – a company markets their brand a certain way, so a professional should use similar techniques. Considering the prevalence of social media, mobile technologies, and other web service, the underlying concepts of online personal branding are always changing. (For example, LinkedIn a major player in personal branding had 20 million viewers in 2006 and now has more than 300 million viewers.)

I think a personal professional website acts as the centerpiece of an online personal brand. In building a personal website service, I have further conceptualized how to effectively create an online personal brand: using skill sets effectively, infusing various forms of media, and connecting to other platforms. I believe my functional model is refreshingly more simple and applicable in building an online personal brand.

I have been creating websites and web applications since 2006. For the past three years, I designed and coded a mainstream personal website service. I completed one year of coursework towards a MBA at the University of Maryland, and earned a degree in Management Science from SUNY Geneseo. I currently immerse myself with the subject of personal branding and follow the latest trends.

Personal branding excites me because it is an opportunity to define yourself. You find ways to promote yourself to a target audience, which you have the tools to reach – something professionals could not do just ten years ago. You can create new, insightful content – blogs, graphics, and videos – that you publish on various networks. Online personal branding does not cost much, so the only real barriers are time, attention, and commitment.

As you read this book, I hope the takeaways are strategies you use to project and take control of your online personal brand. It has become a requirement and should not be taken lightly. An effective personal brand has the potential to open many doors for you.

Contents

Introduction	7
What Is an Online Personal Brand?	9
Why Should You Manage It?	12
Skill Set	16
Working Towards Mastery	20
Establishing Credibility	23
Aura	27
Branding Strategy with an Aura	31
Create a Slogan	34
Visually Striking	37
Identity	40
Ownership of an Identity	46
Connections	51
Getting Found	54
Brand Experience	57
First Impression	60
Projecting Your Personal Brand	64
Managing Content	69
Accessible on Mobile Devices	71
Understanding How Others Perceive You	75
Behave Accordingly	81
Promotion Versus Prevention	86
Using Motivational Fit	88
Personal Branding Involves Competition	90
Become That Guy	92
Attitude, Connections, Vision, & Presentation	96
Personal Website: The Centerpiece	98
How to Build an Online Personal Brand	103
Employment Evaluations	109
Leadership: Personal Branding	113
Millennials	116
Millennial Survey	121
A Personal Brand and a Company Brand	125
Maturation Process of a Personal Brand	133
Personal Branding Challenges	139
Conclusions	143

Appendix A: Diagrams	148
Appendix B: Personal Branding Books	150
Appendix C: Millennial Branding Survey	153
Appendix D: Personal Branding Tips	155
Appendix E: Glossary of Terms	159
Notes	162

Introduction

In my last book, *A Skills-Based Approach to Developing a Career*, I presented a methodology centered on the development of a skill set throughout a career (Frischmann, 2013). A professional thinks about skills as he or she plans and builds a career, and there is utility in presenting and validating a skill set; it is a snapshot of a professional's capabilities and is highly searchable. However, there is more to a person than simply a skill set; there are also personality traits, values, interests, and connections. To capture these other elements in this book, I define and discuss my interpretation of an online personal brand.

There are a few reasons why you must proactively manage your online personal brand. First and foremost, you already have an online personal brand, whether or not you take control of it (a point made by all the experts); therefore, you should "commandeer it" (Schawbel, Me 2.0: Build a Powerful Brand to Acheive Career Success, 2009). For example, someone searches your name in Google and views the search-engine results page ("SERP") to learn more about you. They form an opinion of you based on what they find. Second, you build an online personal brand to differentiate yourself from your peers by presenting your skill set, sharing aspects of your personality, and building relationships. Third, when you effectively project a personal brand, you demonstrate vision and maturity by knowing how you want to be perceived and doing something about it. Finally, it makes sense to orchestrate your personal brand when you are passively or actively seeking employment, as it gives potential employers a holistic view of you.

Like a skills-based approach, my interpretation of online personal branding coincides with my work in developing a mainstream, personal website service. I assert that a personal website acts as the centerpiece of an online personal brand. A personal website has an interface that allows you to present your skills and utilize all sorts of media to effectively portray your brand. You also own a unique domain that is the central node for your interactions on the Internet and establishes an identity, something you can reference in social-media profiles and what will appear when someone searches for you in Google.

In this book, I discuss the three elements — skill set, aura, and identity — and how they overlap. Because the Internet itself is one vast network connecting us in so many ways, it is important to corral what is being said or published about you into a unified brand whenever possible. I will discuss how to project your personal brand through networks.

What Is an Online Personal Brand?

Personal branding is a popular topic in professional circles nowadays. It is defined as the process whereby people and their careers are marked as brands. Most experts distinguish personal branding as being similar to companies branding their products or services and suggest utilizing the same marketing techniques as companies. In *Me 2.0* and *Branding Pays*, two highly successful books on personal branding, the authors pitch the idea of creating a personal marketing plan. Consider yourself the product and potential employers or clients the target market. Find ways to promote your skills, abilities, values, and personality to a target audience (market) by using a value proposition and effective networking.

Overall I think comparing personal branding with product branding is somewhat effective; however, I think there are weaknesses in basing your branding strategy solely on this approach. First, presenting skills and personality traits should be rooted in something empirical, such as test results or assessments. Second, a single value proposition might be an overgeneralization of how you want to be branded. Third, it takes a lot of maturity to accurately predict a target audience. Finally, there are far more professionals than companies in the world, so I think it is much more difficult to base personal branding on product differentiation.

With online personal branding, the focus is how you are perceived on the Internet and related networks, such as social media, content providers, and public records. After viewing your LinkedIn, Facebook, and Twitter profiles, one gets a powerful glimpse into your professional and personal experiences. They might view content you publish in Scribd, WordPress, YouTube, or Instagram. They might find out where you live, places you've worked, and your contact information. All of this is accessible to anyone searching your name with Google or Bing. The goal of online personal branding is to channel all of these stimuli into a unified message, where you control your reputation and how others perceive you.

I have come up with a functional model for online personal branding in a simple formula:

skill set + aura + identity = online personal brand

A skill set represents your functional or rational value. The definition of a skill set is the combination of skills you have acquired throughout your employment, education, and other experiences. A skill is an attribute required to complete a particular task. You can publish your skill set through various web services, including LinkedIn, Facebook, and Google+ social-media platforms, Monster.com's job board, and a personal website.

The complement to this functional presentation is your aura, or how people perceive you through your personality, appearance, style, and charisma. An aura represents your emotional value. Probably the best way to understand how others perceive you is to conduct an interview with peers and supervisors.

The final element of an online personal brand is an identity — a representation of your connections and how you are projected onto networks. A primary objective is to harness your digital footprint to exude a cohesive brand.

Why Should You Manage It?

Most experts say you should take control of your online personal brand because it is already out in the public domain. They say anyone can search on your name in Google and get information about you. Google search results include links to your social-media profiles, places you blog or post content, and background information about you. (And I argue that the first link should be your personal website.) One company, Brand Yourself, offers a service to help you take control of your Google search results by strategically placing desired links at the top. Getting your target audience to click on prioritized links is a good start, though I suggest getting deeper by managing actual content.

Content published online is often accessible to the general public and almost impossible to permanently delete. (Applications hosting your content create backups, and it is easy to download an image or copy text from websites.) Moreover, comments you make get read. Someone who accesses your Twitter handle can view all of your tweets and see your connections. When you think of personal branding, consider how someone would perceive you after reviewing content, regardless of whether you meant for him or her to have access to it. As one author puts it, "The Web is not anonymous nor can anyone control its flow of information" (Richter, 2013).

> There was a Wired article about the impact of a single tweet. A woman attending a PyCon conference overheard two men say an "indecent pun," and she responded by tweeting their pictures and what they had said. Her tweet went mainstream. She and one of the men lost their jobs from this interaction. With nine thousand followers on Twitter, she should know every tweet holds significant weight and must be in synch with her personal brand (Metz, 2013).

It is beneficial to manage an online personal brand if you are actively or passively seeking employment, particularly if you expect potential employers to search for you online. It is advantageous to have recruiters access a multidimensional resume with rich content and media, rather than the standard text MS Word resume. A personal website and/or social media acts as the conduit for delivering this added content, which might include videos, images, documents, blogs, and portfolios. Developing an online personal brand projects a multifaceted image of you to potential employers.

As you build an online personal brand, you want to make it accessible to recruiters. Publish your skill set—the functional, rational part of a personal brand—on a personal website, social-media profiles, and job boards so that recruiters can find you. Once they find you, they can learn more about you. This engages the *pull approach*, where you *pull* recruiters to you, and this is powerful (Frischmann, 2012).

Professionals looking for employment make an impact through a personal website or social media. The opening story in *The Resume Is Dead* is about Matt Epstein, who created Googlepleasehire.me to get the attention of the big web service he was targeting. His splash page got the attention of four hundred thousand unique viewers and landed him eighty interview offers (Wang, 2012). Other professionals are placing ads on Facebook and Google to attract recruiters.

Even if you are not necessarily seeking employment, online personal branding is an effective way to differentiate yourself from your peers. Essentially you want to become *that* guy or *that gal* for a defined ecosystem. You might be the *SEO* guy, the *web* gal, or the *IP law* guy. The ecosystem might be defined based on a community you live in, your college-alumni network, or people you know. Once your reputation gains traction, show career vision—something extremely valuable.

Finally, an online personal brand represents you when you connect with others. Since everything is online, you are forced to connect with other people on various networks. This often involves an online first impression, which all future interactions are based upon. Your online personal brand should exude how you want to be perceived and make your audience want to connect with you. It does not matter if you are an introvert or extrovert, you must make the necessary connections to advance your career. In a way, it is easier for introverts to make connections online because it does not require face to face time and they can respond and post messages after contemplation (Clark, Personal Branding for Introverts, 2013).

Millennials do not yet understand the importance of managing their online personal brand, despite being inundated with the newest web applications. Social-media companies, such as Facebook and LinkedIn, have web services that increase in value as the number of connections increases, so their objective is to grow the network. The number of personal connections of a profile is prominently shown and, in many ways, reflects a person's status. Millennials get enamored with the network effect and do not think about the identity aspect when using these applications. However, since millennials utilize social media widely and frequently, it is imperative they consider their presence on the different applications collectively.

The sophistication and depth of an online personal brand depends heavily on a person's current or expected profession. Some professions do not require personal branding, but most do. Many accountants, lawyers, and doctors want to emphasize *prevention* as part of their brand—an assurance they will not create problems. Many leaders, marketers, and designers want to emphasize *promotion* as part of their brand—an assurance they can gain influence. To reach a large, intended audience, writers create profiles across many social-media profiles and manage them to achieve maximum exposure. A personal website should act as the centerpiece of an online personal brand for all professions.

One author writing to professionals in their twenties summarizes the importance of an online personal brand, he says "Building your brand with a legit online presence amplifies all of your existing personal branding, networking, job-searching efforts X 177" (Angone, 2013).

Skill Set

Related to a personal brand, skill sets represent your functional value. Someone reviewing your skill set gets a snapshot of your capabilities. After seeing your skill set validations—certifications, references, and samples of work—he or she has a true glimpse of what you bring to the table. There are a few advantages to thinking in skill sets.

Skill sets are highly searchable, both externally (from a different platform) and internally (from the same platform). LinkedIn and Monster.com have built powerful search engines (Recruiter and Power Resume, respectively) based on skill sets. SkillPages built a whole web service that allows recruiters, potential employers, and consultants to search desired skills within a certain area. Internally speaking, skills should be linked to experiences the way tags link to content (as is common in blogs). I have established this linkage on a personal website service I developed. Once you link skills to experiences, you can search a skill, and all the related experiences will appear.

Skill sets have been adopted by most major social-media services—LinkedIn, Facebook, and Google +, job boards—Monster.com, and personal website services. Ideally, it would be beneficial to port a skill set from one platform to another. This is precisely what Mozilla has constructed in their online badge infrastructure—something they call *a backpack* (Mozilla). Portability of skill sets would help avoid redundancy and confusion. Moreover, a standardized list of skills and accepted definitions would be beneficial to employers, education, recruiters, counselors, and all professionals.

Skill sets are easily manageable. Most professionals have between ten to twenty skills in their skill set. (In my LinkedIn profile, I have sixteen skills.) There are five ways to present them: tagging, listing, explaining, demonstrating, and summarizing. And there are many ways to validate them. You can have a coworker or supervisor endorse you (a very popular feature on LinkedIn), provide a work sample (according to a survey in *A Skills-Based Approach to Developing a Career*, this is the most effective way), or become certified from a third party.

Like personal branding, developing a skill set is a lifelong commitment. Here are a few reasons why. First and foremost, the velocity at which new technologies are being adopted requires you to learn them as they relate to your skills. Fortunately, there are various new learning channels that allow professionals to continue building skills without having to get a college degree. Online courses are transforming continual learning, which educator William Bowen says is "the educational equivalent of taking booster shots" (Bowen, 2013, p. 44). Mozilla's online badges open up less traditional learning channels by providing a platform for validating skills. You can learn skills or build knowledge on your own and then receive an online badge to certify you have done this properly.

Second, a new requirement for the modern-age professional is to be well versed in soft skills. This is something Seth Godin alludes to when he says you need to become indispensable and not simply a cog (Godin, Linchpin: Are You Indispensable?, 2010). In *Promote Yourself: The New Rules for Career Success*, Dan Schawbel says, "You're going to need a lot of skills you probably don't have right now." He goes on to say that soft skills are more valuable than hard skills (Schawbel, 2013). (Something I do not entirely agree with because I think it is an over generalization. It really depends on your career. Nevertheless, soft skill are essential for success.)

Third, whenever you make a career transition, thinking in skills gives you the advantage of assessing what skills you already possess and what skills you will need to move forward — a far more efficient, effective approach than thinking in degrees.

I think there are many compelling reasons why you should base your career planning and development on your skill set (some of them mentioned above). One big reason is that it forces you to think about building a combination of transferrable and technical skills that thread through your personal and professional experiences. Transferable skills are ones that can be used across subjects and disciplines. Technical skills are related to a specific discipline.

Thread A Skill Set Throughout Your Life

Primary Education (1-8 grade)
Build a foundation of reading, writing, and math skills. Start assessing core-compentencies and passions, and a parent and teacher guided plan of a desired skill set.

Higher Education (Traditional degrees)
Plan the combination of transferable and technical skills needed for a career. Build related skills and concentrate on aptitude and retention. Start the process of presenting and validating skills.

Alternative Education (Apprenticeships, MOOCs, and Online Badges)
Build technical skills required to fulfill a particular job function.

"My Ideal Job"
Utilize skills built througout your life to make an everyday contribution. Enjoy what you do, be stimulated, and add value to those around you. Make your skill set a precious commodity.

Secondary Education (9-12 grade)
Build skills needed to get into a college or university. Use personalized and active learning to stimulate growth. Introduce technical skills to STEM prodigies.

"My First Job"
Start applying your skills on the job. Build 'soft skills' not easily taught in a classroom. Learn methods in applying technical skills.

Further/Continuing Education
Continue building your skill set throughout your life. Commit to taking online courses, watching videos, reading latest news, and writing a blog, social media, etc.

Working Towards Mastery

One requirement of the Information Age is that professionals are going to have to build relevant skills throughout their career. The rapid adoption of new technologies is the main reason why. Professionals are expected to maintain a proficiency with their skill set as new methods and applications are being introduced into their everyday work. Let's take the example of a teacher.

Teachers are now expected to incorporate online learning platforms and social media into their teaching methods. Both technologies are revolutionizing the learning experience altogether. Online learning platforms have made significant headway in the past ten years. Clayton Christensen predicts that by 2019, fifty percent of all K-12 courses will be online (Christensen, 2011). One of the compelling reasons to use online learning platforms is it is a big step towards personalized learning and mastery, something highly coveted by educators.

Some teachers were educated in a particular discipline (like math or science), and others were educated to teach to a classroom (those majoring in education). Regardless of their past education, teachers are now required to learn how to use online learning platforms. This is a challenge because it involves fundamental changes in teaching. All of a sudden teachers have feedback loops, which tell them the effectiveness of their teaching. Rather than having a stack of paper quizzes to bring home, teachers rely on the platform to instantaneously grade quizzes for them; scores are aggregated and tabulated, so teachers can make headway based on the results.

So if you are a mid-career teacher, you will be trained to use these new applications and methods. Moreover, this becomes an ongoing commitment. You will have learn about the latest trends by taking online courses, reading articles and blogs, and/or participating in social media with influencers in the subject. Building skills has become a lifelong commitment.

Another profession that requires continual skill building (which was less of a requirement ten years ago) are doctors. New equipment and robots and the release of so much information online forces doctors to keep abreast of the cutting edge technologies. The proper use of diagnoses tools might save a patient's life. Of course, any professional who uses technology on a regular basis will be faced with changing applications, methods, and knowledge related to their skills.

With regards to a personal brand, you want to effectively define the skills you are working towards mastery in. These few skills signify your essence. You want to show that you are always working to improve your expertise with these skills: list education and employment experiences and show a progression, how you are always working to get better; use demonstration; and provide insights in blogs and social media.

Part of mastering a few skills also means not learning or unlearning other skills. You want to project a strong, focused personal brand so avoid diversifying or diluting it by trying to be a jack of all trades, over committing, or not properly targeting an audience (Montoya, 2009). Of course, you will have to build skills required for your career and sometimes to address weaknesses. However, with mastery, you want to hone in on just two to three skills that you build and validate throughout your career.

In The Rise, Sarah Lewis says about mastery: "Masters are not experts because they take a subject to the conceptual end. They are masters because they realize that there isn't one. On utterly smooth ground, the path from aim to attainment is the permanent future" (Lewis, 2014, p. 33). Devoting a large swath of your life to master a few skills is a powerful message about your personal brand.

Establishing Credibility

As I mentioned earlier, a skill set is the most grounded element in my online personal brand model. An aura is subjective and based on perceptions. The best measure of the effectiveness of an identity could be the number of connections and followers in your networks. However, there are accurate, rational ways to assess a skill set: an assessment, demonstration, online badges, and testimonials.

One way to verify competency with a handful of skills is to take a test, whereby upon passing, you earn a certification, award, or license or simply a score. Usually there is a third-party organization that is responsible for creating, administering, and grading the test; this arms-length transaction further legitimizes the credential. Many professions require earning a credential gained from passing a test to effectively conduct business; some of them include: lawyers, accountant, and stockbrokers. Most graduate schools require that all candidates take a test (GMAT, LSAT, and MCAT) and, in many cases, the results weigh heavily on their chances of being accepted into the program.

Perhaps the most powerful way to establish credibility with your skill set is through demonstration – let your audience draw their own conclusions regarding your expertise. With the advent of the Internet and social media, in many cases, demonstrating a competency is possible and expected (especially when you create your own content); all you have to do is create a file – video, graphics, spreadsheets, articles, presentations, slide shows, web pages, etc. – then simply share a link to the file. If you create a lot of content, you will be expected to provide a portfolio of your work; graphic designers, web developers, or media curators are often asked for their portfolio. Recent college graduates should share samples of their coursework. Finally, to demonstrate you have insights in a subject, you might moderate a blog and/or social media account.

Online badges are an exciting, new way to validate skills. Mozilla spearheaded the development of an infrastructure to disseminate online badges. There are a few reasons why Mozilla's online badges are the buzz. First, they can be used to validate just about any skill. The issuer creates a rubric and badges are issued based on the results of whoever takes it. Second, any company or organization can issue online badges; the only requirement is creating a Mozilla account. Essentially, the issuer's reputation determines the value of the badge. A major implication is these credentials compete with more traditional credentials; there are alternatives to a college degree. Third, online badges are accessible at all stages in a career so it boosts continual, lifelong learning. You earn a degree in computer science and then earn a Mozilla badge in Java, for example. Third, the badge has a graphical interface that is portable across platforms. So it is easy to earn a badge and post it on your website. Finally, Mozilla verifies the accuracy of the badge.

References and endorsements are the traditional way of validating skills. Getting a reference to provide a testimonial of an accomplishment is potent way to validate skills. Just as potent is having a reference tell a story about their experiences with you. The story teller injects humor and emotion, which helps the listener get to know you on a personal level. To get testimonials and stories online, you can quote your reference in text, create a video, or provide a link (with some prompting) to contact them directly.

With online personal branding, you want to make sure you validate all of your skills. Skill sets represent what you are capable of accomplishing, so it is important to back up what you say you can do with evidence. Whenever possible, demonstrate and put the onus on your audience to assess your level of expertise. If you have earned a credential, then place it prominently on your personal website or LinkedIn profile; make it part of your tagline. Publish your online badges. With your LinkedIn profile, make sure your connections are endorsing your top skills.

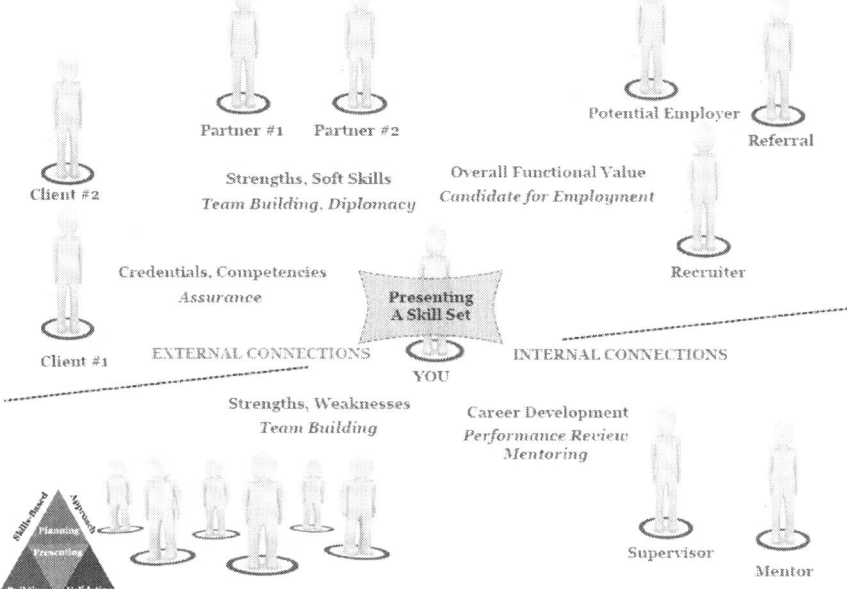

Aura

Aura: *a subtly pervasive quality or atmosphere seen as emanating from a person, place, or thing.* – dictionary.com

An aura is the least tangible element of online personal branding. An aura captures how others perceive you after they review content about you online. This includes content you publish and have control over, such as your personal website, LinkedIn profile, or Facebook profile. You do not publish some of the content, and you have little control over it, however, there are strategies to manage this content too. Because an aura is based on a perception, who visits your website and social media profiles and why comes into play. Take control of this perception; one branding expert calls this skill: "impression management" (Mobray, 2009). Developing an aura is analogous to developing a business reputation in the traditional business sense, without the face-to-face interaction.

Appearance is important. Offline, you pay close attention to your dress attire and grooming. In business school, I remember thinking about what to wear to every event. You are always leaving an impression, and you want to establish consistency. With online personal branding, this relates the style, layout, and aesthetics of your content. Think about how much companies pay graphic designers to get this right on their websites. Once someone visits your personal website, you have less than a minute to make a first impression and develop an intrigue to learn more about you. Moreover, you want have your look unified across your online presence (to the extent you can control it).

Everything you say and do makes a difference. In building a reputation, you want to be liked by your target audience. In many situations, it plays a bigger role in your success than skills. With online branding, how you craft your content is key: following etiquette (Twitter has a lot of unsaid rules), infusing personality, and connecting to your audience. You also want to show you can think on your own—an increasingly sought after attribute in this information age. Another thing to keep in mind when publishing content online is to assume it never goes away. Content is stored on servers, which are frequently backed up offline; all documents, e-mails, pictures, and videos are retrievable. In *Branding Pays*, Karen Kang says, "Deliver a 360-degree brand—a clear and consistent delivery of your brand through all communications, gestures, and actions" (Kang, 2013, p. 124).

Since an aura is based on perception, the best way to understand it is to directly ask people from your target audience what they think of you. Have a sit-down meeting, teleconference, or online chat with an associate or supervisor with the sole intention of understanding what they think of your current online presence. Tell them it will take no more than twenty minutes. Ask them to review your personal website, social-media profiles, and any links accessible from a Google search. Do they perceive your online presence like you are hoping or expecting they will? If not, how do they perceive you? Do they have any recommendations? I guarantee you get some valuable insight regarding how others perceive you. One step further is to have a 360-degree interview, where you have a sit-down, face-to-face meeting with someone you know personally and ask them a list of questions about their perceptions of you (Clark, Reinventing You, 2013).

A personal website is the ideal platform upon which to develop an aura. You can utilize various forms of media. If you are an early-career professional, consider creating a short, five-minute video to introduce yourself. If you are mid- to late-career professional, you might have a blog where you share insight. Either way, use media to share aspects of your personality. This will allow you to infuse your style into the content. Think about the color scheme of a template, the look and feel of menus, and a preferred layout. A visitor is going to have a knee-jerk reaction to the style and aesthetics of your website. Finally, you have more control over content. With a personal website, you can write an elevator pitch that shows your charisma, enthusiasm, and values. Even though you are online and not face to face, you still infuse context that adds a human element to your online personal brand. This is impossible to do with a resume and difficult to accomplish with a social-media profile. But when you have full control of a personal website, you can tell a story with a video, graphic, or pop-up text and respond through a chat, texting, or e-mail.

Using media that is most appropriate, you want to tell a definitive, personal story about you. Think about ways you can piece together professional and personal experiences into a message that flows and allows for an audience get to know you better (Cijo, 2014, p. 78). Characterize important people in the story – almost suggesting them as future references. Find ways to cultivate an emotional connection with your audience by injecting elements of humor, overcoming adversity, or rallying a team.

A well-known marketing guru, Bryan Kramer recently came out with his H2H concept (human to human, rather than business to business or business to consumer) and, in his book, notes, "Humans understand and process information in context…Content is important, but context is HUGE" (Kramer, 2014). Build your online personal brand by providing context to buttress your content so that your target audience gets a deeper understanding of who you are — your aura.

Branding Strategy with an Aura

I suggest employing a branding strategy as you develop your aura. Creating an aura is not as grounded as presenting and validating a skill set but intricate and subjective. Try to capture a prevailing opinion of your personality and presence. Here are some suggestions for your branding strategy (this is not much different than a strategy a company might employ).

First, identify your target audience. Who is part of your ecosystem? Make a list of your current clients, associates, and partners and potential employers. How are you trying to influence them? This is very important because you may take for granted what you are trying to accomplish or how important perception is in winning over your audience. If you are a web designer, you must win over clientele with a sharp, stylistic website. Otherwise, you will lose business, regardless of your skills and credentials. In this example, you want potential clients to get the impression that you are detail-oriented, creative, and tech savvy. So as your work on your branding strategy, make a note of each group in your target audience and the impression you want to leave with them. Later, as you get feedback from your target audience, learn what impression they actually have of you.

Second, try to solicit a response from your target audience whenever possible. A deeper understanding of the impression you leave on people will give you an edge when trying to differentiate yourself from your competition. An aura is cloaked in perceptions, so try to understand them. Here are some suggestions for getting feedback: use a focus group, provide a quick exit survey on your personal website, and ask point-blank questions about what people think of you. Compare their responses to your own expectations.

Third, reflect on some key questions about who you are and what you are trying to accomplish with the aura element of your personal brand. What do my soft skills say about my emotional value? Since soft skills are social, they relate to your functional and emotional value. You might want to impress an audience with your team-building skills or your compassion and empathy.

How am I a solution to a problem? A strong sales pitch usually solves a problem. Think of ways your unique combination of skills, values, and interests can solve a problem for a potential employer. (Take this approach, and I guarantee you will get a job.)

What is my value proposition? This is a strong elevator pitch. Use media and content that summarizes who you are in less than a two-minute glance of your personal website.

Finally, in putting everything together, try finishing the phrase "I have a presence of…"

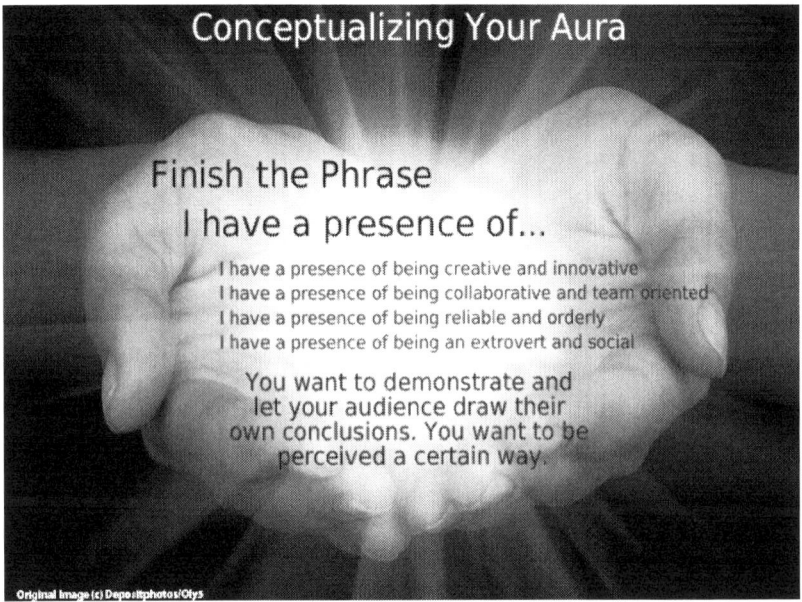

I like the metaphor Linda Ries bases her book *Visual Hammer* on: "You need two things to build a brand—a visual hammer and a verbal nail. And the nail comes first" (Ries, 2012). She is talking about company branding, but it works for an online personal brand too.

To clarify, a stunning, visually appealing personal website is the hammer, and an elevator pitch on the website is the nail. Tying the two together is a powerful way to influence your target audience.

Create a Slogan

Finding a way to represent your emotional value in a slogan is a powerful way to reach your audience. A slogan – analogous to a mantra – is the 'heart and soul' of your brand (Marrs, 2012). Of course, companies develop mantras (implicitly or explicitly). A good example is with car manufacturers. Here are some examples of one word phrases car manufacturers have established with their brands: Volvo – safety, Volkswagen – economy, Mercedes – performance, Toyota – reliability, Cadillac – luxury, and GM – utility. In *You Branding*, Mark Cijo states "Many experts even call personal branding the 'you business', and that's an accurate assessment" (Cijo, 2014, p. 85).

As you develop your brand, try to summarize your message into a few words and make it personal. You can then decide if you want to promote your slogan implicitly or explicitly. Ways you can deliver your slogan implicitly are through content and/or appearance to get your message across to a viewer; make sure you put the content in a prominent place. Make it a focal point in a similar way an artist tries to draw your eyes to a particular place on a painting. For example, say your message involves compassion, you might use a video demonstrating your compassion in a personal or professional setting or a story depicting how you helped someone. Put it on the homepage of your website so someone visiting it cannot overlook it. Ways you can deliver your slogan explicitly are by using it as a tagline in a heading, keywords in a promotion campaign (Google AdWords, Facebook, and/or Twitter), as part of your domain name (**www.ideaactualizer.com**), and by tagging content with it.

The primary reason for developing a slogan is to differentiate you from other professionals. Moreover, it is something your audience remembers and associates with you on an emotional level. Something visual also helps your audience recollect their impersonation of you. It is unlikely you pick a slogan that totally standouts from everyone, there are too many people in the world. But hopefully, there are few competitors with similar slogans in your target audience. And you may consider further differentiating your slogan by adding another dimension to it. Related to the car manufacturer example above, Tesla has successfully carved out its own niche defined in two words: performance and eco-friendly.

Think of something personal you can draw on. Let's take an example of a computer programmer. He or she will have a difficult time differentiating from other programmers, especially on an emotional level; the responsibilities of programmers are predominately functional. In their personal lives, programmers might cut the stress by hiking, sailing, volunteering, or playing sports in their free time. They should incorporate these experiences into their brand. The idea is to not only share personal experiences with a target audience, but also find a way to tie it together with the other part of the slogan.

This is very common on a Twitter profile, where you have one hundred sixty words to define who you are and attract others to connect with you. I have read profiles where someone with similar professional interests of mine, also shares that he or she is a parent, participates in hobbies or sports, or helps a social cause. As you make connections with people, the heavily active Twitter participants say Tweets are all about connecting in a personal way (whether or not they are doing it for professional reasons).

To illustrate this idea of a slogan, let me explain mine. I try to identify with two words: reliable learner. I express my slogan implicitly in the content on my website and in the taglines of my Google+ and LinkedIn social media profiles. On my website, I emphasize that I am a continual learner – always taking courses (MOOCs or at a university) – through a timeline application. In my social media profiles, I say I am 'driven to actualize ideas'. A few things to notice. First, my slogan does not say what I do professionally but rather describes me in what I feel is a personal way. In a later chapter, I talk about a concept of being *'that guy'* that is meant to capture your professional contribution – so it is different. (I try to be that 'web developer' or 'personal brander' in this context.) Second, there are ways to subtly tell your audience how you want them to perceive you. And, depending on your audience, they might appreciate this added level of sophistication. Finally, summarizing yourself in two words makes you self-aware. Throughout my life, I have always prided myself to be reliable. Being a learner was my top strength in a Gallup Strength Finder test and after self-reflection I agree with this assessment; it clearly fits me.

You should come up with your own slogan. To come up with one, reflect on your personal and professional experiences, take personality or strength tests, and/or ask someone who really knows you well. Once you have one, find a clever way to deliver it your audience.

Visually Striking

Find striking pieces of content that will be etched into the mind of your target audience. There is the cliché phrase: a picture is worth a thousand words. Why? Because pictures are memorable. You can recollect an image, far better than a narrative. Pictures can also often be used to portray a metaphor, which adds another layer of sophistication to your content. For example, in this book, I have used the following metaphors in my graphics: an aura as a light, juggling content, linking aura and skill set as food, and applying to jobs with portraits.

Graphics require spatial rather than attribute processing. It refreshing to process a sharp graphic with only basic wording. According to one study, ninety percent of information transmitted to the brain is visual, and *visuals are processed sixty thousand times faster in the brain than text* and forty percent of people will respond better to visual information than plain text (Vaughan, 2012).

An image or video has the potential to add a soulful dimension to your online personal brand. You can add something that is aesthetically appealing based on something meaningful to you. For example, if you like to travel, you might share a picture of you interacting in a foreign culture (similar to something you might find in a National Geographic magazine). This could be a powerful way to say you are a global citizen. In *The Rise*, Sarah Lewis summarizes the influence of imagery in the viewpoint of Frederick Douglass: "'The whole soul of man' when 'rightly viewed' as 'a sort of picture gallery a grand panorama' contrasting the sweep of life with the potential for progress in every moment" (Lewis, 2014, p. 91).

Visual media – graphics and video – is easy to share with an audience. All you have to do is to publish the digital file in social media, on your personal website, or in the cloud and then link to it. To the contrary, when you share text, you have to worry about its appearance and layout (fonts, spacing, etc.). On Facebook, videos are shared "twelve times more than links and text posts combined" (Vaughan, 2012). Pinterest has carved out a niche as the social media platform to share visual content; it has been embraced by companies to enhance their brand. Likewise, use Pinterest to increase exposure of your personal brand.

I started blogging in June 2012. In early 2013, I decided to follow common practice in other blogs by including a graphic with each post. My response rate increased and I received many positive comments on my graphics. In fact, I think the graphics are what my audience remembers most from my blog posts. Conveying an idea in a graphic is a powerful, effective way to reach your audience. It is fun to think of how you want to translate a six to eight hundred word essay into a graphic to further get your point across. Moreover, it is an opportunity to hit home with a metaphor. Finally, a graphic and the first few sentences are often what appears when you share content in social media.

Social media profiles bank on one visually appealing graphic. Each of the big four social media profiles give you an opportunity to publish a background graphic, the single most important characteristic to differentiate the appearance of your profile. I highly suggest thinking strategically as you develop your graphic.

As you create a striking graphic, make sure you put a personal mark on it and it radiates your personal brand. Rather than going to a stock photography website or using a generic graphic from a service provider, create your own. If you cannot create your own graphic, find one that will not appear anywhere else. I do not understand why places that sell graphics or website templates advertise their popularity. Why would you want to buy the same graphic everyone else is using? LinkedIn is offering access to generic background images as part of their premium membership profile. The whole point is to differentiate, and considering you have one chance with appearance in a LinkedIn profile, why would you choose one of their generic images.

There is an opportunity to share something personal about you when you create your own media. You might take a picture or video while you: participate in a hobby, spend time with your family, or finish an accomplishment. A picture or video might be about something you value, find interesting, or deeply connect to. The idea is to promote your personal brand. Give your audience a reason to want to connect with you. Prompt them with something to talk to you about after they connect with you.

Producing a video has many similarities to producing a graphic but is more complex; you can deliver a WOW factor with a video. Creating a video requires choreographing actions, constructing a setting, and writing an effective script. It is important to consider each of these elements as you develop a video. Your typical viewers are inundated with watching video clips, so a well-conceived video stands out; viewers remember a striking video and may watch it again. (I can easily recollect a handful of homemade videos that left a lasting impression on me.)

Identity

An identity is how you are represented across networks: the connections you make, networks you join, and content you publish on these networks. With the ever expanding reach of the Internet, it is becoming more important to understand how to manage your identity across all web platforms. I suggest having a personal website that acts as the primary node for your interactions—something you can link to from other web services and maintain ownership of the content. For example, I link back to my personal website from my Facebook, Google+, and LinkedIn profiles, so if someone wants to learn more about me, he or she can go to my personal website, and I have more control over his or her experience. I also recommend using social-media networks for their intended purpose only, to avoid duplicating content. There are some things to consider with managing your identity.

Establishing an identity is your responsibility, so you are your own advocate. Social-media services concentrate on building vast networks and do not necessarily think about the identity aspect of their services. Decisions social-media companies make often aim to expand their network. Once dominance of a certain type of network is established (and you have to become part of it), they develop the identity aspect of their service (often at a premium price). LinkedIn got traction with their network and now charges a premium service for added features, for example. In addition, many of these social-media companies have you relinquish sole ownership of the content you publish and mine profile information that they pass onto third-party marketers.

This is how they offer you a free service. For these reasons, social media services cannot champion both their network and everyone's identity – it has to be one or the other. Therefore, you must take full control of your online identity — the third element of your personal brand.

As said before, it has become a requirement to join social-media networks. The number of connections you have gives you status. There is a rush to get 500-plus connections on LinkedIn, a thousand followers on Twitter, and over a thousand Facebook friends. Unfortunately, sometimes the quantity of connections carries more weight than the quality of connections. You can now easily purchase connections. All of a sudden, you can have hundreds of connections — many of them people you have never met before. When you visit a colleague's profiles, you always know how many connections they have because it is prominently placed on their profile. Likewise, the content you post has status attached to it. How many people read, liked, and shared your post is very prominently displayed. All the connections and content you publish are a reflection of you and your personal brand.

Most of us join a network, become enamored by the network effect, and quickly make connections. Joining social media is often based on social motives: "to satisfy needs for affiliation and social connectedness" (Labrecque, Markos, & Milne, 2011). Later we react to how we are being represented out of necessity. It takes maturity and restraint to avoid this pleasure of connecting. Nevertheless, professionals should first proactively build an identity — a personal website and a collection of social-media profiles — and then make connections. In a later chapter, I talk about how and why you should use a *bottom approach* as you develop an online personal brand.

Like offline connections, it is important to make online connections. The difference between the two is sharing. With most networks, as you make connections, you also provide access to your own connections.

Always think before publishing content on a network. Common advice is to be mindful of what you publish to avoid personal content being viewed in a professional context. A potential employer, for example, may conduct a Google search on your name. They can then view your digital footprint: social-media profiles, digital files, and contact and background information. In addition, whenever possible, you want to maintain full ownership of your content. This is one reason why I suggest having a personal website, where you can claim sole ownership of the videos, images, and articles you put on it.

The identity element plays a crucial role in your online personal brand. Collectively, the networks you join, connections you make, and the content you publish should be considered as part of your brand strategy. It should not be an afterthought or a reaction. Be patient as you make new connections, and carefully calibrate how you publish content. Establish your identity first, and then establish your networks.

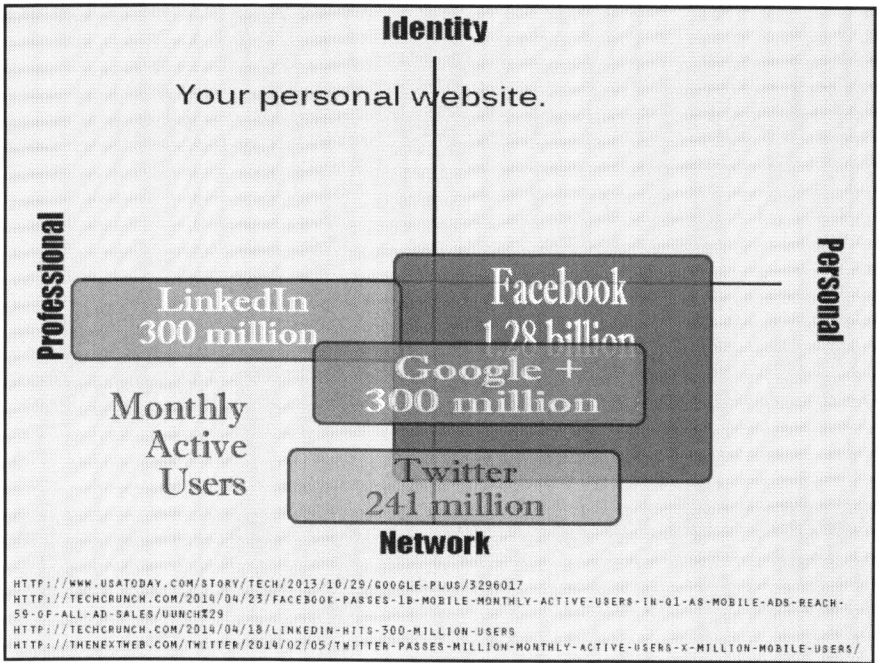

What is clear in the diagram above is how Facebook is currently the behemoth of social-media networks. It has 1.28 billion monthly active users, more than Twitter, Google+, and LinkedIn combined, though the other networks should catch up because each has a differentiated use and there is less space for Facebook to grow. To reach a larger audience, it makes sense to use Facebook as part of your online personal brand. But it is built as a network to connect family and friends, so be cognizant of the personal material you post on it, and remember that some content is accessible to a public audience.

LinkedIn is growing fast. With three hundred million monthly active users, it has a sizeable audience. You must use LinkedIn with your online personal brand. It is a network built for professionals: reputable influencers post great content, associates and clients connect with you and endorse your skills, and recruiters and potential employers can search out specific skills and find you.

Google+ is a hybrid, having both personal and professional uses. You should set up a Google+ profile, as Google wraps the interface with all of its other applications, including its powerful search engine. Like LinkedIn, Google+ also has a good following of influencers posting great content, but, unlike LinkedIn, you can connect with them (though they do not have to follow back). Google+ has about the same number of monthly active users as LinkedIn. Getting your profile and associated content indexed by Google searches is a compelling reason to use this service. (In the future, I predict Google builds a search function for indexing personal websites.)

Finally, you have Twitter. You can use Twitter for personal and professional reasons, but usually there is a delineation based on an account. (Twitter users often have two accounts: a personal and professional one.) Twitter is a great way to make connections and stay on top of the most recent news related to your profession, but profiles are brief and not a strong representation of identities. These are the big four social-media networks that will survive and which you should have a beachhead in.

There are many other social-media platforms, and some grow so fast that they could be on par with these four very quickly. You should have the same strategy when joining any network. Figure out the basic concept behind it, and fashion an identity based on its key features. Remember to link back your personal website whenever possible. Once your identity is firmly established, start making connections. Do not get wrapped up in the network effect and make connections too hastily.

Ownership of an Identity

A theme I talk about throughout this book is ownership of a professional identity, which holds significant weight as part of your online personal branding. The four main elements of a professional identity that you want to take ownership of include: a domain name – your address on the Internet, your search engine results page ("SERP"), valuable content – you intellectual property ("IP"), and the design and layout of main landing page – a personal website. Ownership of your professional identity has its privileges.

Owning a domain name is necessary for a couple of reasons. You have certain rights. It is published with ICAN – a worldwide directory of domain names. In a way, a domain name becomes another personal identifiable characteristic of yours – like a cell number or an address. Domain names are portable across all hosting and cloud platforms. So you can change providers of these service whenever you choose. This makes it enduring. You should keep the same domain name throughout your career.

Nowadays a SERP has become a big part of your online reputation, so you need to take control of it. Of course, technically you cannot own the results of a search in a major search engine, so what I am suggesting is conceptual. But a SERP is something you want to command (to the extent you can). There are ways to publish your own content and links, get reputable people or companies to link back to you, and push unfavorable links lower in the rankings (so they are off of the radar when someone searches on your name). This is the underlying concept behind a service offered by BrandYourself.

As I have discussed earlier and will do again, you want to understand ownership rights to your intellectual property. With your more valuable IP, you should maintain sole-ownership rights to it. Many of the free social media service make you share ownership rights to your content. This might not be a big deal for much of your communications, but could be dangerous with IP you have invested significant time and financial resources into. In Facebook's service agreement (as of June 2014), it says Facebook has a legal right to use your IP royalty free, worldwide, and sublicense it.

Finally, in a broader sense, you want to have ownership of your identity. First let me clarify how you own a professional identity. You build a website. You purchase a domain name, hosting, and utilize a platform to construct the website. All these services are paid for (whether it is packaged together by one service provider, or separately among many service providers). In their service agreements, you do not relinquish any ownership rights regarding your intellectual property. The development platform you use to build the website allows for you to design and control all the real estate on your website down to the pixel; it is all about you. Finally, you use search engine optimization ("SEO") to place your website and content high in Google rankings. I argue that in this situation, you are taking ownership of your professional identity.

An alternative situation would be to use a profile in social media as a professional identity. This is what LinkedIn wants you think. In fact, it is what their CEO Jeff Weiner said in a recent interview: "Invest in your profile, invest in your professional identity is absolutely critical to your success" (Sandholm, 2014). One career expert says: "If you are going to choose only one personal branding tool to invest time in, choose LinkedIn" (Aruda, 2014). I question this assertion. Why would you choose one tool for personal branding considering its importance for a successful career? Wouldn't it be more effective to invest your time in a personal website, something you can use as an identity in all your networks? Do you sacrifice a sense of security investing in a self-contained platform like LinkedIn? The biggest problem in over-representing your identity in social media is that they have already invested heavily in a network. Is it possible for a company to strongly advocate the development of a network and an identity simultaneously? I think a company has to represent one or the other for a few reasons.

A big issue is whether a company can grow a network without offering a free service. The four major free social media networks (Facebook, LinkedIn, Google+, and Twitter) offer a free profile, which is predominantly chosen by its user base. Their networks have grown rapidly because there are no barriers to join. But as discussed above, an effective professional identity is something you own exclusively. Can companies offer a free service without having professionals relinquish rights to their intellectual property?

In addition, these companies strategically put marketing advertisements on your profile page – a distraction to your audience. These advertisements are meant to take the attention off you and to a service offered by a company. If your viewer clicks on the advertisement, there is a strong chance they do not come back to your profile. Finally, these social media companies mine data regarding your personal information and behaviors to third-party marketers.

What matters here is the behaviors part. A new company, Five, has developed a tool with functionality to analyze your posts in Facebook, Google, and Twitter and determine your personality types, which is just a glimpse of what social media companies are learning about us (Hardy, Your Personality Type, Defined by the Internet, 2014). With your own personal website, you should have some basic privacy and copyright protection. The links visitors click on are only revealed to you.

Other issues arise when you establish your professional identity in a self-contained platform. If you over-invest in a single profile, your brand might "face substantial losses in the event of member migration to a competing company" (Labrecque, Markos, & Milne, 2011). There are also boundaries with self-contained platforms. First, you cannot modify the underlying structure of the profile; you must rely on the service provider to set the parameters of your profile. For example, Twitter recently updated their profile and LinkedIn followed suit with their profile. The hoopla was in allowing users to add a background and a bigger image in their profile (Troung, 2014). That's it!

Second, you are going to want to publish content in one place and be able to reference it many different places; this allows for you to maintain exclusive rights to it. Third, it is not possible to create code blocks that can be accessed across different platforms. I see this as being an important part of a professional identity. You want access to the underlying HTML and CSS code (not the scripting per se); one platform that currently gives you this type of access is Wordpress. The younger generation is being introduced to coding; it is being taught to kids, and modifying underlying HTML and CSS is supported in all of the major browsers. Finally, with a self-contained platform, you are going to have very limited access to the database storing all your information.

The impact of social media services cannot be overstated; they have transformed the world we live in. To effectively use their networks, you have to create a profile so do it for the web service's intended purpose. A LinkedIn profile, the connections you make, and getting found by recruiters is a necessary part of your online personal brand. So construct your LinkedIn profile by adding resume content, listing skills, and publishing content you are comfortable sharing in the public domain. However, you also want to construct a personal website that acts as your primary professional identity – something you own.

Connections

A significant part of online personal branding is represented by your connections and relationships, especially in the socially connected world we live in today. Your connections might endorse your skills, challenge your insights (commenting in blogs and posts in social media), socialize on a personal level, give you Klout, and conduct business with you. For better or worse, the number of connections you have influences your legitimacy in each of the four big social media services; all of them plaster this number on your profile so everybody knows how popular you are.

Here are some strategies to expand your reach and increase the number of connections you have. First, join online groups and/or circles. Most of them are open to the public and are accessible via social media. Second, comment on articles and blogs that interest you. Authors are forced to moderate, so they are compelled to read your insights. Third, tap into your current network. Alumni networks, family ties, and communities are usually very supportive of their members. Fourth, create content an audience cannot ignore. There are many free ways to disseminate content. If you create something valuable, then viewers will respond. Fifth, participate in Twitter. Getting a Twitter following for the average professional is predominantly based on a daily time commitment. If you Tweet frequently and interact with others, your follower base grows. Finally, make yourself accessible. You should create a personal website and social media profiles, which you manage to rank high in Internet searches. Give potential connections the opportunity to find you in the first place.

The quality of your connections should not be ignored. (Personally, I prefer having fifty 'quality' connections over two hundred 'mass audience' connections.) LinkedIn puts up a wall regarding anonymous connections; you must have some prior relationship before inviting someone to connect with you. Although, there are still ways to poke holes in the wall. The decision to connect with an acquaintance in LinkedIn is about not only the acquaintance, but also their extended network (which you would have access to). So if you want to block access to your connections or have no common ground with a connection and their connection base, then do not add them as a connection. Twitter has two sides regarding a response to an anonymous person following you. One side says to only follow back if you foresee having a mutually beneficial relationship; one side says you should always follow back – who is so high and mighty that they cannot follow back.

Beyond the credentials, creating quality connections involves creating an open, two way communication channel. Popular marketing guru Seth Godin describes a quality connection: "(it) involves a complex swap of information, expectation, and culture" (Godin, The Icarus Deception, 2012, p. 44). Identify connections who you want to designate as 'quality connections', then make sure you build an effective relationship with them. This means responding to direct messages with them, commenting, favoriting or liking their articles, blog posts and Tweets, and sprinkling personal information about you in your communications. Avoid making a mistake – grammar and spelling, poorly conceived thought, or an out of character post – with these connections.

Being successful in the Information Age requires being socially connected, which is why it is a necessary component of an online personal brand. Connectedness is pervasive in just about everything you do. Connections help you get a job. Connections get an audience to pay attention to you. Connections communicate with you and give you feedback. Connections are human in an increasingly automated world. Connections give you business.

As you project your online personal brand, think about how to connect to your audience. Establish a connection base in each of the four main social media services and, again, establish connections based on the intended purpose of the service. LinkedIn is a professional network where you generate insights, endorse skills, and get found by recruiters. Facebook is a personal network where you connect with people who have traversed through your life. Twitter is a way to connect to other professionals with very little disclosure – you have only 162 words in your profile. Google+ is a way to create circles – sub networks.

Getting Found

According to my diagram, getting found is the intersection of an identity and a skill set. An identity represents your presence on networks, including social media and the Internet in general. A skill set is highly searchable externally and internally, so it is what you publish in various platforms. Getting found requires presenting your skill set so that it can be searched on from within a network. It should be a coordinated effort to gain maximum exposure to a target audience. (GoDaddy, a popular web-hosting company, recently added a new marketing tool called Get Found.)

In *A Skills-Based Approach*, I discuss five ways to present your skill set: explaining, demonstrating, tagging, listing, and summarizing. Tagging is effective for searching and viewing lots of content. It has the same purpose as assigning key words to a blog or article, where someone searches a set of key words to retrieve related content. You can assign skills and some auxiliary words (such as a "technology," "method," "application," or "level of expertise") to any block of content—a paragraph of text, an image, or a video. That content appears when someone searches for your designated skills.

You can incorporate this concept of tagging skills to your personal website. Since the content is individualized and professional in context, you can tag skills to much of it: samples of work, accomplishments, videos, blog entries, etc. Other platforms should include the functionality to tag skills to content. I would not be surprised if LinkedIn weaved it into personal profiles.

The idea of getting found works with other ways of presenting a skill set on social-media services, job boards, and recruiting platforms. LinkedIn has a search engine called Recruiter, where recruiters can search for a skill set. (It happens to be their big revenue generator. Recruiters pay a big subscription fee to use it.) A LinkedIn profile has an interface where you list your skill set, which can be endorsed by people in your professional network. You can also summarize your skills in a tagline. Google + has a profile where you can summarize your skills. I think Google should provide a search that indexes personal websites, where interested parties can search on things like skills. Facebook allows you to add a list of skills to your profile and will probably add some sort of search mechanism at a later time. In the context of personal branding, you should think about how you establish an identity and present your skill set in all networks.

The biggest benefit to getting found is having access to recruiters, whether you are actively or passively seeking employment. (Some argue you should always make yourself accessible to recruiters, not matter how secure you are in your job.) Publish your skill set on the networks recruiters regularly use to find talent (like LinkedIn and Monster.com); remove the burden off of you to search for recruiters. Let them conduct a search and review your skills and contact you if necessary. If they do, you have the opportunity to share with them the last piece of your personal brand: your aura. Otherwise, you can review their bread crumbs to learn more about the effectiveness of your representation. This is possible in LinkedIn, as you can see how many times you appeared in searches and who looked at your profile.

Of course there is also a benefit in engaging clients and/or partners who are trying to learn more about your credentials; let them find you on LinkedIn or through a Google search. Clients are usually looking for assurance, so, by providing them to access to the presentation of your skill set on a network, you are allowing them to evaluate your level of expertise. This may or may not have been something covered by your company. Nevertheless, the company sold them on your product or service, and now it up to you to sell them on you. Partners are an extension of your team, with the added requirement of diplomacy. It is worthwhile to let your partners have more access to you so that they can learn more about your core competencies or how you make the most impact.

Brand Experience

The technical term for the combination of your rational value (a skill set) and emotional value (aura) is "brand experience." In my model, brand experience represents the same, without the projection onto a network (identity). The objective of a brand experience is to optimize your online presentation so it accurately portrays the whole you. In *Branding Pays*, Karen Kang says, "The brand experience is the overall experience that we want to deliver when others come into contact with our brand" (Kang, 2013, p. 90). As you develop a brand experience, you want to use online content to establish a powerful, accurate link between your rational and emotional values. I have three food metaphors from experts to help describe this link.

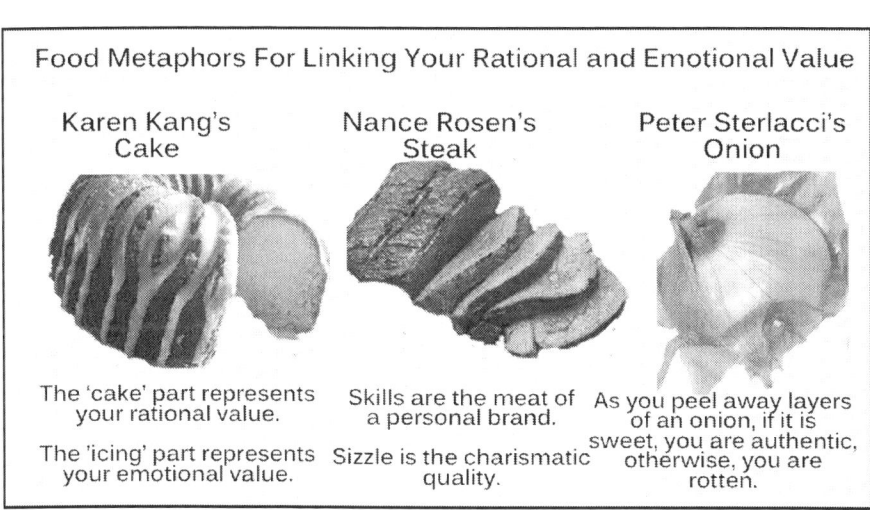

In *Branding Pays*, Karen Kang uses a cake metaphor to describe the brand experiene. The cake is your rational value. It is the foundation and takes up the crux of space. The icing is your emotional value. It has a major wow factor. For many, the icing on a cake has the biggest influence on its flavor and, therefore, determines its likeability. But you cannot have a cake without the actual cake part; icing by itself is too sweet and unpalatable. Sometimes you can get away with having cake without icing.

When combining your rational and emotional values, it is crucial that the link between the two is authentic. You do not want to have a skill set that does not compute with your aura. Otherwise, you lose trust and credibility. For example, an individual who presents a skill set in sales management does not compute with a shy, reserved aura. A good way to think about it is to consider the peeling of an onion. As you strip away the layers, if the onion remains sweet, you are authentic — otherwise you are rotten (Sterlacci, 2013).

There is no getting around the importance of your rational value captured as the presentation and validation of a skill set. When a recruiter posts a job position, he or she lists desired qualifications. As candidates apply, like clockwork, a recruiter checks each qualification against a candidate's capabilities. You cannot get through without the necessary credentials. As Nance Rosen puts it: "Skills would be the meat of your personal brand. Sizzle is the charismatic quality" (Rosen, 2012).

How do you link your rational and emotional values? Come up with a brand strategy where you evaluate each piece of content you publish and assess its functional and emotional values to be sure the two align cohesively. For example, start with your personal website. Read the content and think about what it says about you objectively (in a way that is similar to a resume). Use a checklist to make sure you present and validate each of your skills. Then step away for ten minutes and come back. This time, do not read everything, but rather skim through the content. Look at the style and how the content is laid out. Write down your perceptions on likeability, personality, and presence. Finally, compare the results of the checklist and the perceptions. Do they coincide? Do they reinforce each other?

A brand experience can be a powerful way to establish influence with your target audience. It is deeper and more involved than sharing your capabilities. When the presentation of your rational and emotional values is in synch, it gives you significant credibility. Moreover, with so much published content out there, it has become a requirement. Graphic designers can spout out all they want about their skill set, but if they are not convincing with emotional-value-driven content, it is unlikely they reach their true potential, for example.

First Impression

With the popularity of social media and connecting online, you are going to make personal connections with people you have never and will never meet face to face. Moreover, these connections might have a strong influence on your career; they might be a coauthor on an article, a partner in an organization, or a long-standing client. As you develop a branding strategy, you must consider your online first impression. According to my diagram, this is the intersection of an aura and identity. What do people think about you after visiting your personal website without a careful examination of your skill set? In the *10Ks of Personal Branding*, the author summarizes the importance of a first impression: "the first impression you make is the lasting impression others take" (Mobray, 2009).

In the first five seconds, they will make a snap judgment of you based on the style and aesthetics of your website. This is probably why many of the new personal website companies emphasize they will help you create "stunning" websites. One company's name says it all: Strikingly.

The focal point of your online first impression is a professional website because it gives you flexibility with aesthetics, use of media, and content. It is hard to do much, stylistically speaking, with a social-media profile, so you are better off making your personal website a landing page. Simply add a link to your personal website in your profiles. Of course, there is a chicken-and-the-egg problem related to generating enough intrigue to get someone to click on the link in the social-media profile. Technically, the first impression is based on what is found on the social-media profile; nevertheless, you can still make an impression once someone gets to your personal website.

The home page of your personal website becomes a primary reference point. It makes a huge impact on whether you generate intrigue to learn more about you, which is usually your objective. You should invest enough time crafting the home page so that it is impactful and you impress. There are a few things to consider as you build a home page for an impactful first impression.

Make sure you spend enough time working on the style and taste of your personal website. It should suit your profession. Lawyers, accountants, and consultants may use stark colors and a formal structure and menu — as if they want to avoid making a mistake. Graphic designers, web developers, and marketers should find something creative that exudes what is currently most appealing (slick menus, animation effects, etc.) — as if they have something to prove. Your style "tells an instant story about you — whether you are serious or fun, traditional or progressive" (Demarais & White, 2005, p. 41).

The primary content on the page should be direct and free of clutter. Similar to a good painting, the viewer's attention should be drawn to it immediately. Consider telling a story or demonstrating a core competency. If it is text, it should be short, concise, and in a large font. With other media, make sure it serves its intended purpose. A well-choreographed video shows passion and creativity. An interactive app, such as a time line, works well too. You have a few seconds to get your viewer to digest the information and decide to learn more about you.

In most cases, you should keep the subject matter positive and avoid edgy material or diatribes. If you feel compelled to include this type of material, save it for another section on your personal page (just keep it off the home page).

Provide easy, clear navigation to other pages on the website. Make sure your menu is prominent and that there are hyperlinks in your content. Once you get someone hooked, you want to give ample opportunity to learn more about you. Similarly, foster further communication by providing them with ways to contact you: an e-mail address, chat interface, or phone number.

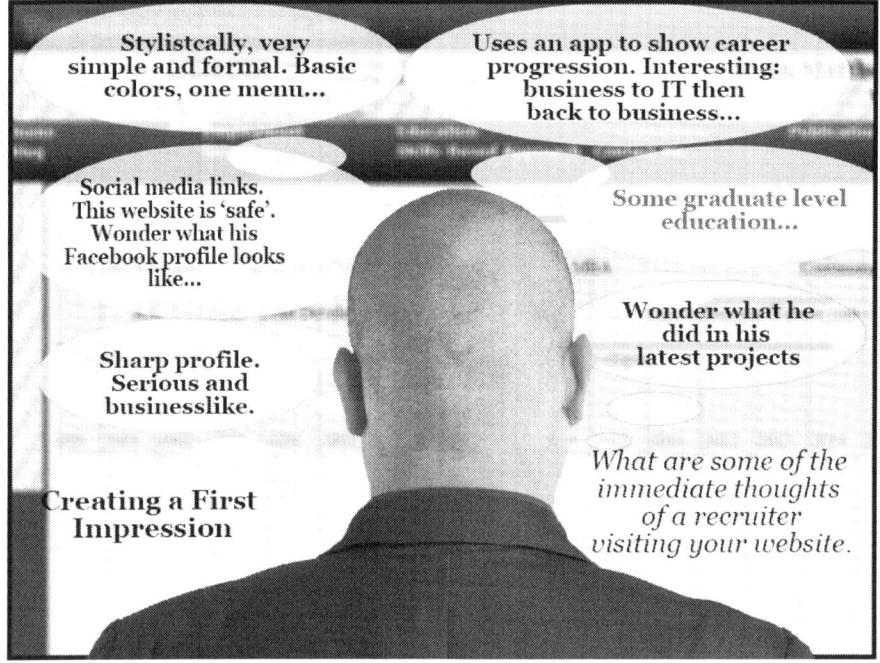

Finally, I have one last point regarding online first impressions. A popular fad is to create catchy taglines, advertisements, and domain names to attract the attention of potential employers, which is otherwise almost impossible to do. It is unlikely you will get a company like Google or Microsoft to review your functional value (a full representation of your skill set). Google had over one million job applicants in 2010. The gimmick is to show ingenuity and creativity that grabs one moment of a recruiter's attention; hopefully you generate intrigue and get them to click on a link to your personal website. This could be a Facebook ad, a Google Adwords campaign, a Tweet with a particular tag, or on any other network where you can reach your intended audience. It is hard to say if this type of self-advertising will last much longer because, unless it becomes a norm, it has a spamming effect and gets to be annoying. Nevertheless, it is worth considering because of the potential payoff.

Projecting Your Personal Brand

One fundamental aspect of an online personal brand is that you can take ownership of it and project it on social media, cell-phone apps, a personal website, and other networks. This means proactively managing content, rather than posting it online and then later reacting based upon how it affects others' perceptions of you. Understanding how joining a network and publishing content there affects your personal brand should be a precursor. Expanding your network in social media is enticing because the number of connections you make sometimes establishes a reputation, and the network effect becomes fun; there is a "natural inclination to preen and collect 'likes'" (Tulathimutte, 2013). Social-media companies know about the network effect. They also know that, according to *Reed's Law*, the value of their network grows exponentially based on the number of users (Wikipedia, n.d.). But overexposure and ineffective content can have serious implications on your personal brand.

This is why I suggest a bottom-up over a top-down approach. Every time you join a new service, conceptualize how it affects you. First, think about how the profile defines you. What does it say about your capabilities and who you are? Second, think about the content you are sharing with the service. Who sees the content? Will you be sharing personal or professional content? Does the content expire? Third, think about ways to deliver your personal brand. Can you link to your personal website? The basic idea is to think about *you* before *us* and ensure that you think about your personal brand as you join new services. If you are already part of some networks (I am sure you are), ask the same questions above, and react to what is already out there.

To get started with a bottom-up approach, you might think of your online personal brand in terms of assets and liabilities. Take an inventory of your assets and figure out the best way to leverage them. Assets might include your valuable IP, standout experiences, core-competencies, a knowledge base, and/or strong connections and relationships. To leverage these assets, you accentuate them on your personal website and profiles, maintain ownership privileges to them, and make them accessible in the right circles. Of course, with liabilities, you want to minimize their influence. For example, if there is an unwanted link high on your SERP page, you find ways to bury it.

The problem in joining networks and making connections haphazardly is that you are sharing these connections in an ever expanding network, so it is unclear who has access to what. In LinkedIn, you can have a hundred of your own connections that reach out to several thousand others. Any time you make connections, you get a glimpse of all their connections, and they get a glimpse of all yours. Think about how valuable contacts were just ten years ago. They were kept sacred in a Rolodex. In many professions, a person's connections determined his or her value.

There are a few dangers in publishing content indiscriminately over a network. A commonly talked about one is the dubious delineation between personal and professional content. What you post on Facebook, in many cases, will be seen in a professional context. A public Facebook profile is easily accessible via a Google search. It is also very easy to rip content. For an image, all one has to do is use a Windows Snipping Tool to take an image from any website (or even more simply, right click and save it your computer). Finally, with the Internet, content never goes away (except some of the new mobile apps, which disappear after a certain amount of time). The best way to protect yourself is to think about how the content reflects your authentic self and personal brand.

Combining connections and content also has serious implications on your personal brand. As you make connections and post content, you almost have to assume everyone in your network will view your post. Sometimes a clever innuendo, pun, or joke is well received in your audience, but sometimes it is not. Sometimes you get responses; other times there is utter silence. But probably the worst is a message with bad grammar or spelling or that is simply not well thought out. A few bad posts can seriously damage your professional credibility, and with so many people vying for attention, it can damage your career. In LinkedIn, there is no way to heal a bad reputation; it is actually quite frightening. As career expert Peter Montoya says in *The Brand Called You*: "Every time you fail, you dent your brand slightly. Enough failures – enough contradictions of you promise – and you'll wreck your brand" (Montoya, 2009).

With a bottom approach, always consider your identity element as the top priority. As you make connections, take your time, and be patient. Consider rolling out your social media profiles and personal website in stages – alpha, beta, version 1.0, etc. – in a similar way companies do. For your alpha release, provide access to your online personal brand only to a tight few colleagues, friends, or family who know you well and will give honest and direct feedback (that is in your best interest). For your beta release, expand your audience to include clients, partners, and coworkers who you interact with on a regular basis. When you are ready, release it to your target audience as version 1.0. You will of course continue to add new versions as your online personal brand deepens and begins to crystalize.

Think about your behaviors as you project an online personal brand. Do you respond too quickly to emails without enough reflection? Has content you published been thoroughly reviewed? Good behaviors garner respect with your audience (Dalla-Camina, 2014). Finally, as you publish content, always consider it as a reflection on you, and be careful with personal material. Think of content as a permanent record.

Social Media
Connections
LinkedIn, Google+, Facebook, Twitter

Personal Website
The centerpiece
You own a domain name and all of the content.

PROJECTING AN ONLINE PERSONAL BRAND

Social Media
Blogging
Wordpress, Blogger, Tumblr

Social Media
File Sharing
YouTube, Flickr, Slideshare, Scribd

Managing Content

Part of projecting an online personal brand involves managing your content and putting it into context. It is astonishing how much content we create and share on a given day, and more importantly, the expectation our audience has that we do so. Twenty years ago (before social media) these expectations did not even exist. Today many professions require that you participate in social media fifteen minutes every couple hours. If you have a blog, experts recommend writing two to three entries a week, and of course, moderating it daily. Since it is possible to create and share visually appealing media (such as video, graphics, and infographics), professionals are expected to have this type of content too.

There are many ways to disseminate content. It is possible to create and send content via mobile devices. Apps are used to share the content. There are numerous web services that allow for you to save content in the cloud; some of them include DropBox, Microsoft OneDrive, Adobe Creative Cloud, Amazon Cloud Drive, and Google Drive. You can then change the settings to allow others to access it. You can also use a personal website as a repository for much of your content.

Social media services allow for you to share your content on their networks. Some standardized uses include, sharing: personal pictures in Facebook, videos in YouTube, and professional articles in LinkedIn. I recommend using social media services strictly based on your intended purpose; this will help avoid putting content in the wrong context. For example, do not share personal pictures in LinkedIn. Generally speaking, all of your LinkedIn connections see your content and many of them do not know you on a personal level (and some have no interest to).

One caveat of these free services is you relinquish ownership rights to the content, which could be dangerous to your personal brand if you are not careful. Probably unlikely, but imagine Facebook using one of your pictures in their marketing advertisements (it is within their rights).

In terms of your online personal brand, you want to collect and control access to your content (which you should consider as your intellectual property), put content in the right context (little personal content in LinkedIn, for example), understand ownership rights to the content, and leverage your best content by making it accessible. If you have something valuable to contribute, you want to get it out. From a utilitarian perspective, it is your duty to get the content into the hands of your audience so they benefit from it. To do so, publish your content in well traversed, connected web services: LinkedIn, Google+, Twitter, WordPress, Pinterest, and Scribd (Pappers, 2014). Prized content is a powerful reflection on you and your capabilities.

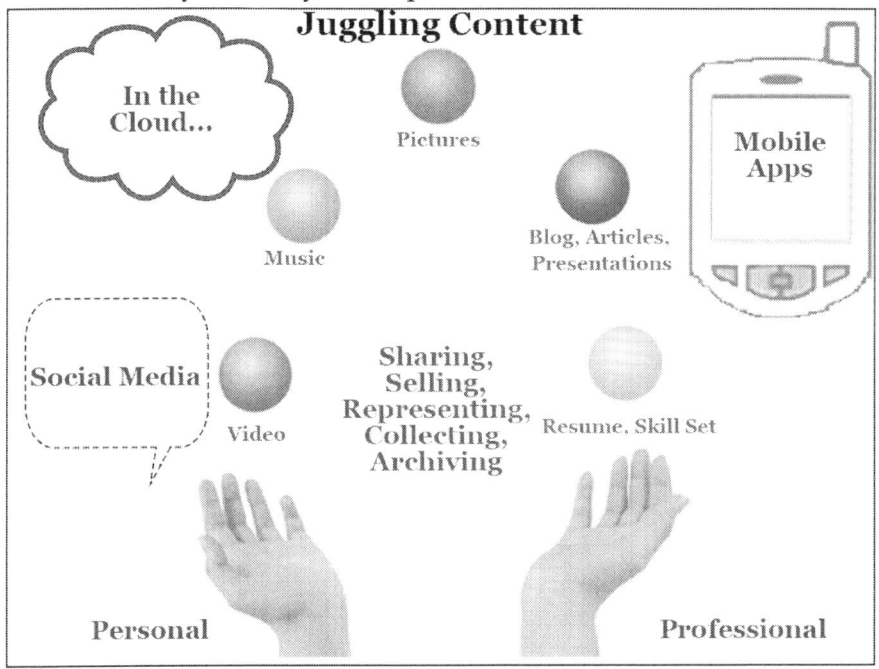

Accessible On Mobile Devices

The use of mobile devices – tablets and cellphones – has exploded in the past few years. In fact the four big social media services claim to have mobile usage on par with computer usage. Facebook says that 1 billion of its 1.28 billion monthly active user base accesses via a mobile device (Wagner, 2014). Twitter says 198 million of its 255 million monthly active user base accesses via a mobile device (Protalinksi, 2014). There is no doubt mobile usage will surpass computer usage in frequency and time spent in the near future. (I call the next generation, Generation Z, 'mobile natives' because almost all of them will be brought up using mobile devices.) With online personal branding, the heavy use of mobile devices and apps means you must: establish a mobile presence by making yourself accessible on an increasing number of mobile applications, provide frequent bite-size communications, and publish a mobile version of your personal website.

The four big social media services built mobile applications (apps) to access the key features available via their traditional web service. The main implication regarding your personal brand is the frequency of access to your communications and content in social media. A CEO of a content distributor sums it up: "We used to interact with personal computers daily, for two to three hours at a time. With laptops, we started interacting three to four times a day for 20 minutes each. Mobile phones made that into sessions of two minutes, 50 times a day" (Hardy, Writing in a Nonstop World, 2014).

In the Information Age, for many professions, you are expected to communicate frequently throughout the day – especially if you are trying to establish yourself as a thought leader; mobile devices make this requirement easier. You can communicate anytime and anywhere from a mobile device. If you have not already, I suggest downloading and trying each of the apps from the four big social media services. You might become a mobile convert and predominantly use the mobile app (like I have with Twitter). Moreover, you become familiar with how these social media apps work and appear on a mobile device.

The use of apps is becoming the *common interface* of the future. In Windows 8, Microsoft created a hybrid interface based on traditional Windows and an app way of doing things, for example. Related to personal branding, you are going to want to understand the popular new mobile apps for two reasons. First, you might have to sign up and create an account to effectively use the service (something like Instagram). You can then make connections and share content. Second, you might have to use an app out of necessity. An app such as SnapChat becomes a way of communicating because you want to make your content disappear after it has been viewed. It is refreshing to share content and not having to worry about it popping up somewhere else and being taken out of context, which indirectly affects your personal brand.

There are dramatic differences between a mobile and web optimized website; the two big ones are screen size and load time. When you create your personal website, you want to make sure you have an effective mobile version – it cannot be an afterthought, not anymore. I serve one of two different versions of my website based on the device my visitor is coming from; although the data and content is fed from a single source. My main website is graphic intensive, utilizes a timeline application, and fits on the page well; so I am taking advantage of a faster computer processor and a larger screen. I deliver a complete representation of my online personal brand. My mobile website is basic; it has text and no graphics. I essentially use it to present and validate my skill set.

You can understand how your audience is accessing your personal website by using Google Analytics. It collects all the relevant statistics including accesses by mobile devices, operating systems, and screen size. You will discover that many of your visitors come from mobile devices.

You might consider developing a mobile application based on your personal website (which is different than a mobile website). The basic concept is to pull the content and data from your personal website to populate the application. There are two kinds of mobile applications that are becoming popular in the online personal branding space: mobile resume apps and content sharing apps.

To conclude, the basic concept is to take your current online presence and make sure it is accessible on mobile devices. You should have your personal website optimized for mobile devices by either serving two versions of it – one for computer access and another for mobile access – or making your personal website responsive – appearance and content changes depending on the device. Using mobile devices also makes it easier for you to communicate frequently throughout the day – a requirement in many professions.

Understanding How Others Perceive You

Much of an online personal brand is based on perception: what a target audience thinks about you after visiting a personal website, viewing social-media connections and profiles, and processing all this content about you. Elements, such as your skill set, can be evaluated objectively, but much of everything else is subjective and differs from one person to another. In a way, you want to conduct a "digital brand audit" (Labrecque, Markos, & Milne, 2011). According to the founding father of personal branding, Tom Peters, "Power is largely a matter of perception. If you want people to see you as a powerful brand, act like a credible leader" (Peters, 1997).

To understand perceptions, find ways to solicit feedback about your online personal brand. Provide an exit survey with three quick questions on your personal website to get some insight of impressions. (This can sometimes be annoying, so provide a link so that participation is optional.) In an e-mail, simply ask a colleague what they think of your personal website. After you make a connection (in any of the social-media services), send a direct message, inviting a back-and-forth communication where you can find out what a new connection thinks of you. This is common practice on Twitter. The idea is to piece together these small details to understand you better, and getting this extra feedback will give you an advantage over professionals who are less self-aware.

Another way to get feedback is to have an open-door policy. Tell online connections and visitors to your website or blog that you have an open-door policy. You are willing to accept and listen to unsolicited suggestions and feedback. Tearing down the formal barrier will give you an opportunity to get some real, candid responses from your target audience — ultimately making you much more self-aware. The author of *Emotional Intelligence 2.0* says, "Increasing your accessibility can only improve your relationships — it literally opens the door to communication, even if it's virtual" (Bradberry & Greaves, 2009, p. 194).

Most employers give performance reviews. This is another way you can get some good, candid feedback. Hopefully you get some sort of document written up by a supervisor, manager, and/or coworkers and then meet with them to discuss it. (If not, try to set up an informal meeting or conversation.) This is a big opportunity to learn about your personal brand, so make sure you are ready to take advantage of it. Ask about your current job performance. Are you meeting expectations? Ask about your career development in the short- and long-term outlook. Are there ways the company can help you reach your goals? Finally, ask some of the personal questions so you can uncover those suspicions you might have about yourself. How could you become more likeable? With the project- and team-oriented ways of doing things these days, you might not have the time to really get to know everyone. Understanding your soft skills is arguably more important than hard skills, so at every opportunity, find ways to become more self-aware, socially aware, and relationship aware. Remember that there is a major human element in a personal brand, so you want to: "become authentic in who you are and intentional about how you tell your story" (Gardner, 2013).

With the digital age, there are online logs for all of our communication: e-mails, texts, social-media feeds, and chats. Another way to get a grasp of an online personal brand is to go back and review these logs. Step away, pretend you are someone else, and review these past communications. What do you think of the e-mails you have written over the past month? Are they too formal? Are there grammar or spelling mistakes? If you have a Twitter account, read through all of your recent tweets. Are you forgetting to leave a personal signature on them? Are they boring? Are people responding? I guarantee you get valuable insights by simply reviewing your communications over the past month.

Earlier I talked about using a focus group to flesh out perceptions about you (something Dorie Clark suggests in *Reinventing You*). Corporations use focus groups to understand customer preferences and impressions about their company brand. This is the best way to understand perceptions. Have a sit down at a computer with Internet access to ask point-blank questions about what someone thinks of your online personal brand. Try to limit these questions based on what they have access to online. You might ask: "Does my personal website make you want to learn more about me and perhaps do business together? Does it give you the impression I am creative? What do you think of my public profile on Facebook?"

Teenagers understand the sophistication of online perceptions and conduct informal focus groups. I watched a PBS *Frontline* documentary, *Generation Like*, about teenagers using Facebook. One of the settings included seven teenagers sitting around a table at one of their homes, with each of them holding a laptop and connected to the Internet. They discuss the impact of each other's Facebook profiles and answer some of the following questions: What is the implication if I *like* something? How many views do I get if I post a message or picture? What do you want for your profile to accomplish? What should you have as a profile cover picture and caption?

Arguably, the stakes are much higher for adults because online perceptions have major career implications. Your reputation is paramount, as careers have become more transient. Adults are forced to manage their personal and professional content effectively. The bottom line is that adults should practice some of the same techniques teenagers are using to understand how they are perceived online.

Taking this idea of a focus group a step further, you might consider starting a personal-branding club. It would function like a book club. You meet every few weeks with a collection of friends, associates, colleagues, and neighbors—a branding community—and, rather than talking about a book, one individual and his or her personal brand becomes the focal point of the gathering. Each group member gets his or her own special night, so commit to a schedule like any other club.

The group consists of associates who know enough about each other to share personal and professional insight. I suggest creating a Google+ group for coordinating the meetings (make sure to include a Google calendar). When it is your night to be the target of the group, host the event and (similar to what Ms. Clark suggests with her focus group) provide a comfortable environment with refreshments to show appreciation for people willing to spend their time on your behalf. The personal-branding club has a standard agenda, where there is an orderly way of doing things for each event. The purpose is to brainstorm on how others perceive you, get advice on how to move forward in your career, and simply talk candidly in a nonstressful environment about your career. You are the star for the night.

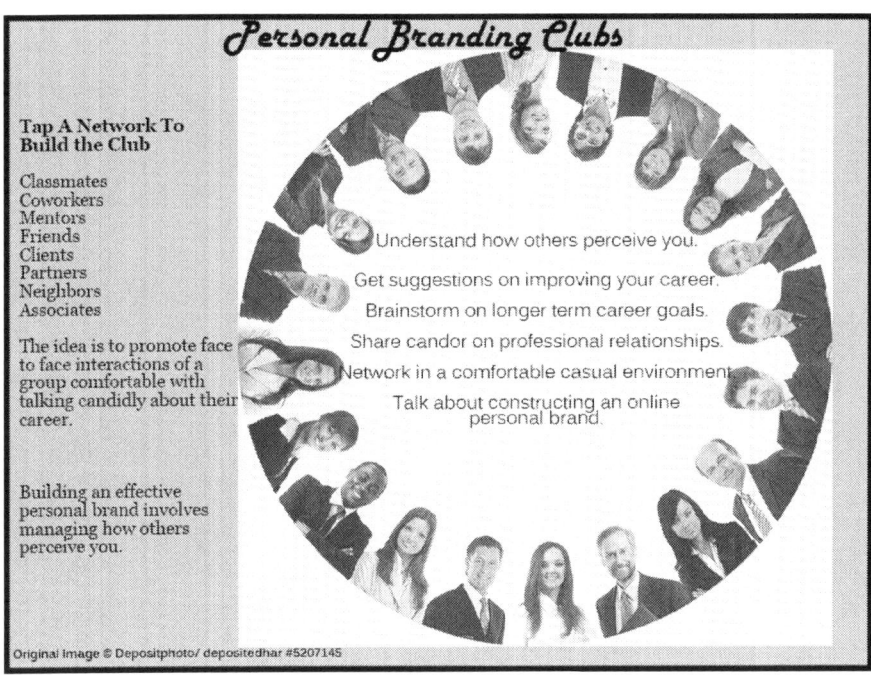

Behave Accordingly

In defining an online personal brand, you lay out a set of expectations so it is important that you behave according to them both online and offline. I am not going to discuss the offline behaviors, so if you want to learn more about them, refer to a personal branding book in the appendix. However, as more of our interactions move online, there are an increasing number of behaviors to consider.

You want to respond to connection invitations in a particular way, perhaps create a *new connections policy* that defines the criteria for accepting connections. Are you always going to accept connection invitations? If not, what do you make your decision based on (whether they have connections already in your connection base, for example)? Like I have already said earlier, do not make connections too quickly.

Specify how many new connections you want to make in a given week and stick to it, then think about ways to get to know them. As you make new connections, try to get to know them by reading their recent posts and then sending them a welcome message that bridges what they have to offer with what you have to offer. In social media, when they provide you with *suggested connections*, read their associated profiles and network before deciding to make the connection.

Consider the frequency of your social media interactions. There are many personal brands that require constant communications in social media, such as brands that have characteristics of leadership, marketing, technology, thought leadership, and public administration. To effectively establish credibility, you must participate in the social media discussions. Otherwise if you do not need a major presence in social media, then still consider the right frequency for your interactions and make it relatively constant.

Create a schedule for disseminating new content. Of course, this schedule varies considerably depending on your online personal brand. For example, if you blog, you want to implicitly tell your audience: "you can count on me to deliver a weekly blog post". There is a big dropout rate for bloggers, so if you can get past the first hump and regularly post a weekly blog, you establish authority and a deeper connection with your readers. Another example is with a painter who posts his or her painting on a personal website. If he or she posts to an online portfolio regularly (every two weeks or so), then he or she generates more regular traffic to his or her website. So even if you create content in spurts, release it your audience in a stream.

Social media experts are trying to capture this in ratios: how frequently you share content you created, others created, and personal updates in your social media steams. A Fast Company article *The Art of Self-Promotion on Social Media* discusses five such ratios. The primary objective is to balance self-promotion with relationship building –avoid being an "attention hog" (Lee, 2014). It comes down to managing the underlying behaviors as most professionals are forced to establish an online presence.

Regarding your communications, consider the three Cs of effective personal branding communications: clarity, consistency, and constancy (Salpeter and Morgan 2013). In emails and social media posts, you want to have a clear voice. Your style and delivery should be uniform in your communications. With the majority of online connections, these communications are the only way somebody gets to know you in a personal and professional way; there are no face to face meetings to clarify things. So it is crucial for connections to feel comfortable with you, something that is only accomplished through normalcy and consistency.

Make sure there is commonality between your personal website and social media presence. Initially when you first build a personal website and social media profiles, make sure they effectively complement each other. Use the same style and appearance (background image, color scheme, and tagline). Your slogan and elevator pitch should be the same. Then, as your brand evolves, make sure modifications to your personal brand cascades across all portrayals.

You want to be adaptable to others' perceptions of your personal brand. Establishing your personal brand is not analogous to proving a thesis, but rather modifying a perception. So you want to always solicit feedback regarding the effectiveness of your branding efforts.

Finally, try to show enthusiasm as you project your personal brand. Be proud of you: who you are and are becoming. Let your target audience get a glimpse of your vision and how you are different from everyone else in the world.

Online Personal Branding Behaviors

Sharing Content: Steady, Creative, Insightful

Projection: Measured, Social, Proactive

Communication: Clarity, Constancy, Consistency

Soliciting Feedback: Attentive, Adaptive, Openness, Responsive

Inward Expression: Self Control, Confidence, Awareness, Committed

Outward Expression: Assertiveness, Enthusiastic, Assurance, Visionary

Promotion Versus Prevention

As professionals think about personal branding, they think of self-promotion. In a survey I conducted (and discuss in a later chapter), some of the open-ended responses on promotion include: "Everyone is a stalker these days...It's CREEPY... I don't need personal promotion."

I would like to clarify that personal branding is about promotion AND prevention. Professionals sometimes have to balance both or, depending on their target audience, might favor one over the other. A prevention-focused audience wants to hear you are vigilant and competent so they avoid a loss. A promotion-focused audience wants to hear you are creative and insightful so they achieve a gain (Halerson & Higgins, 2013). So depending on your audience, you want to serve prevention- and/or promotion-focused content.

Tom Peters summarizes this concept of promotion and prevention effectively. He says the way you communicate your brand is not only about what you do but also what you do not do (Peters, 1997). So part of what you do not do is preventing miscommunication.

Here are some examples of prevention-focused content:

- Provide references who can testify on your behalf. It is difficult to demonstrate competency and thoroughness with a sample of work, so you need references to describe what you did for them. An accountant cannot provide actual audit paperwork, so he or she uses testimonial from a client, for example.
- Highlight repetition with the goal of demonstrating consistency. A prevention-minded audience feels more comfortable knowing you have performed your duties

many times before—the more times the better. If you decide to have surgery on your foot, you seek a surgeon with a reputation for doing the same surgery on other patients.
- Present certifications demonstrating knowledge. Most professions favoring a prevention focus have certifications and/or licenses (CPA, Series 7, Bar, etc.), so it is important to let your audience know you have passed the requirements.
- Use succinct, results-oriented language. A prevention-minded audience concentrates on the details and reads textual content line by line (what Dr. Halvorson and Dr. Higgins call attribute processing). To illustrate, think about how comparisons are made with tables in Consumer Reports (an example used in *Focus: Use Different Ways of Seeing the World for Success and Influence*).

Here are some examples of promotion-focused content:

- Provide samples of work. It is difficult to capture impact in an explanation, so use a demonstration to showcase your creativity and innovativeness. For example, a marketer shares a portfolio of slogans and/or advertisements he or she created.
- Make the presentation visually appealing. Promotion-driven people are more likely to appreciate the sensory appeal of other forms of expression: audio, video, and images. To convince this type of audience, a web designer wants to be thought of as tech savvy and so uses various forms of media.
- Present awards for achievements. Brandish an award or badge for reaching a milestone and standing out among your peers—something more common for a promotion-focused audience.

- Use inspiring language. A promotion-minded audience concentrates on the big picture and will pick up on the themes of the textual content (what Dr. Halvorson and Dr. Higgins call holistic processing). Create memorable one-liners, knowing this might be the only thing someone remembers after reviewing your content.

Promotion

Stylistically Appealing

this website is stunning, very creative...

Holistic Processing

_____
_____

Demonstration

Portfolio

Awards/Badges

Prevention

Repetition

I have completed this procedure countless times before...

Attribute Processing

- _____
- _____
- _____

Testimonials

... her work is thorough and complete. We were assured the audit...

Certifications/Licenses

Using Motivational Fit

A powerful way to influence a target audience is to convey content with motivational fit. You anticipate the expectations of your audience, and deliver content in a way that increases your chance of winning them over. In the book *Focus: Use Different Ways of Seeing the World for Success and Influence*, the authors define motivational fit: "Motivational fit happens when you create a match between what people want and how they go about getting it — the way they reach their goals" (Halerson & Higgins, 2013, p. 152).

To achieve fit, match promotion-focused people with chances of a gain and prevention-focused people with chances of a loss, as discussed in the book. (In the examples below, the boxes shaded in gray represent a fit).

Finding Motivational Fit

Accountant who prepares tax returns.

		Gain	Loss	
Craftiness	Promotion	Maximize a return or minimize a payout.	There might be penalty if your tax return is not acceptable.	**Thoroughness**
	Prevention	A tax return submitted properly will not cost a penalty.	A tax return not submitted properly may result in a penalty and/or legal problems.	

Marketer who writes company slogans.

		Gain	Loss	
Wittiness	Promotion	Create a memorable slogan potential customers remember. Sales increase twenty percent.	Potential customers are not moved by the slogan. Sales stay the same.	**Attentiveness**
	Prevention	Customers are happy. Sales stay the same or increase.	Customers are annoyed or do not relate. Sales decrease 5 percent.	

Graphic designer who creates website layouts.

		Gain	Loss	
Creativity	Promotion	The layout appears innovative and fresh. Great first impression to website visitors.	The layout appears stale. Bad first impression to website visitors.	**Spotlessness**
	Prevention	The layout satisfies the basic demands of website visitors. There is not harm or loss.	The layout does not satisfy the basic demand of website visitors. They leave the website, there is loss of opportunity.	

Web developer who codes websites and/or apps.

		Gain	Loss	
Innovativeness	Promotion	Contributes insightful ideas, which adds value to the application.	May fulfill basic requirements.	**Proficiency**
	Prevention	Written code is effective and functions the way it is supposed to.	There are errors in the written code. Costs the company to debug and fix problems.	

As you develop your online personal brand, you want to create content that has motivational fit so that you best influence your target audience. Sometimes your audience has a promotion and prevention focus, so include content that addresses both.

Personal Branding Involves Competition

If you think of personal branding the same way you think of company branding, then you would agree that it involves competition. Companies are in fierce competition to reach and convert their target market to customers. You do the same when trying to get your audience to invest in you, whether it is landing employment, influencing a client to purchase your work, or informing your associates as to how you make the most impact.

When you compete as a personal brand, the results are often not apparent, and you may not ever know whether you lost in a finite game, such as landing a job. When a recruiter views your professional website and/or LinkedIn profile, they may never inform you that you were in contention for an employment opportunity. Likewise, you may not know when a potential client considered buying your product. Not knowing how you are competing for a particular job might actually be a good thing.

Trying to differentiate a personal brand is much more difficult than differentiating a company brand because of the sheer number of competitors. There are many more people than companies in the world. That being said, knowing you did not get a job might not be so bad. It could be unnecessary discouragement. Nevertheless, you want to understand your target audience and how to reach and provide value to it. Figure out the best ways to differentiate your personal brand from competing personal brands, so learn about your competitors to do this. Use website analytics, and monitor your social-media networks to understand how successful you are in reaching your target market.

If you do know you lost in a finite game, ask yourself what you could have done to win the game (i.e., get the job). This is called an additive counterfactual, and studies show you will perform better over time if you employ this type of rationale. Here is an example. Prompt yourself with the phrase "If I had only included a targeted cover letter that said this…then I would have gotten the job."

A similarity between the competition a company faces when developing its brand and a person faces when developing his or her brand is that both play in an infinite game in the long-term. There is a waxing and waning relationship where you make a play, and then your rival makes a play, and each move prompts the other to make a better play (Bronson & Merryman, 2013). Many companies competing with each other are in close proximity: tech companies in Silicon Valley, financial institutions in New York, or optical companies in Rochester. These companies battle each other but also create an environment where productivity and innovation flourish; they play in an infinite game, where both sides benefit.

Your whole career can be considered an infinite game. You may not get a particular job (perhaps a loss in a finite game); however, in your career, you can always play another game. Nevertheless, you must know your competitors because, as Mark Cijo says: "No matter what your field is, no matter why you are developing your personal brand, people will compare you with your competition" (Cijo, 2014, p. 87). There are so many resources to make improvements, and your competitors are visible and accessible, whether you find them in social media, blogs, or Google searches. I favor infinite games because everyone wins. I like the way Dr. Daniel Crosby puts it in his self-help book, *You're Not That Great*: "If greatness is worth pursuing, one person's success cannot be tantamount to another person's failure" (Crosby, 2012, p. 32).

Become *That* Guy

One thing that strikes me as I read books by experts on personal branding is that they almost always target an audience of topflight professionals. The author talks about his or her experiences—going to a top college or being uber-successful—and/or shares stories of people who reach similar status. But we all have access to the tools. All it requires is effectively using social media and building a personal website and, if done properly, shows career vision and connectedness. But what many of the experts leave out is properly addressing a target audience, which is why they often cater to the elite. Not everyone can have thousands of Twitter followers or hundreds of LinkedIn connections, and many of us do not have Google or Microsoft on our radar as a potential employer. Yet I think most professionals benefit in establishing an online personal brand.

In *Social Networking for Career Success*, Miriam Salpeter points out the importance of targeting an audience, because "personal branding is not only about you" (Salpeter M. , 2011, p. 7). And this distinction is important: you cannot force a personal brand that is at odds with a target audience. Think of it as a company. No matter how much you promote Coca-Cola to an audience of health advocates, you are not going to be successful. So consider your target audience.

When I think of effective targeting, I think of a phrase an Italian friend says to me about expanding his business; his slogan is "Gotta Guy." He is a handyman, so in his context, it refers to finding someone who can do a particular job locally. For example, it might refer to a plumber, woodworker, electrician, or so on. However, I think it works in a much broader context. You can become *that* guy or *that* gal for just about anything (including many of our service professions): "website guy" or "graphics gal," "SEO guy" or "computer guy," or "bank gal" or "accountant guy." And with the Internet and social media, you can connect to your own particular ecosystem—clients, associates, and employers. Where you live, an alumni network, past or present employers, personal connections, or other societal factors might define the boundaries of your ecosystem. In this way, by using specific targeting, you are not taking a pie-in-the-sky approach but rather a coordinated approach to developing your personal brand. Nelson Wang puts it nicely: "A great brand is only truly powerful when you get it in the hands of the right people" (Wang, 2012).

An example of the *that*-guy approach can be found in regional business-networking organizations. Think about the setup of a typical Business Network International (BNI) group. Each person is guaranteed a unique identity within the group. There is one accountant, graphic designer, insurance agent, website developer, banker, etc., for example. The organization meets to share leads, foster ideas, and build rapport within the community. So with personal branding, take the *that*-guy approach online, and utilize social media to build your network. You might even take the same approach as BNI, a professional referral network ("PRN"), regarding referring new clients. Once you have established yourself as that-guy with an audience, setup an arrangement with your connections to refer you to their connections (and expect for them to want for you to reciprocate) – an excellent way to expand your network and generate new business.

With online personal branding, you may or may not be constrained by the community you live in; nevertheless, you should be able to carve out your own niche. To differentiate in a larger network, you may need to add a qualifier based on your strengths or knowledge base. Still, the idea is to become…*that* guy.

Attitude, Connections, Vision, & Presentation

One way to conceptualize your personal brand collectively is to think about four elements: attitude, connections, vision, and presentation. There is some overlap with the model presented above, but I think this gives an interesting summation of what I have discussed.

Attitude is an important part of career development. Everyone is dealt a set of circumstances and then has an opportunity to assert and establish themselves. There are people who are smarter, more ambitious, and have more charisma than you. Personal branding does involve competition, though in the form of an infinite game—no winner and no loser. So as you progress in your career, think about how you can make yourself indispensable by differentiating. Be the best you can be. Seth Godin talks about becoming a linchpin, and says, "The distinction between cogs and linchpins is largely one of attitude, not learning" (Godin, Linchpin: Are You Indispensable?, 2010, p. 43).

Connections define the much-needed human element of a personal brand. (This is part of the identity element I talked about earlier.) As technology is becoming ingrained in everything we do, interpersonal, meaningful relationships are critical. Human interaction—conversations and sharing emotion—is the one thing robots and computers cannot do well now (and hopefully for quite some time). So while technology has displaced workers due to automation, it has enhanced our ability to communicate. We can now use the Internet, social media, and mobile apps to build a larger number of connections. Always keep your connections close, because they are what separates us from machines and may keep you from being displaced by automation.

Having vision separates the great from the good. This is not to say that you have to have vision to excel, because there are many professionals who live vicariously and do well. However, if you do have a vision, you will stand out from the crowd. It is something Cal Newport touches on when he talks about a "craftsman's mind-set." Identify core competencies, where you derive the most value, and base the rest of your career on developing these skills as "career capital" (Newport, 2012). I also talk about vision in *A Skills-Based Approach to Developing a Career* by suggesting the development of a skill set throughout a career. With personal branding, try mapping your educational and professional experiences into a logical path to demonstrate career maturity. Showing vision is an effective way to command respect.

Presentation is how you deliver your personal brand. With a presentation, define your personal brand and show, explain, and demonstrate how you leverage it to solve a problem. Think of it as a proposal you are giving to gain approval. The best platform for a presentation is a personal website — something you have full control over and can direct an audience to.

Personal Website: The Centerpiece

An online personal brand can be thought of as your digital footprint, though the centerpiece should be a personal website. It is a platform to capture all the elements: skill set, aura, and identity. As I argue in *A Skills-Based Approach to Developing a Career*, a personal website has all the functionality to present and validate a skill set; it supports all the different ways to do so. You have full control over style, aesthetics, and layout on a personal website—at least far more control than a typical social-media profile. This helps you share your aura by infusing personality with flair. You use detailed marketing analytics (Google Analytics) to understand the traffic and behaviors of visitors on your personal website; this gives you a true glimpse regarding the effectiveness of your personal branding efforts. Finally, maybe the most compelling reason, you own a personal website, including its content and a unique domain name. It becomes your address for everything on the Internet. Think of it as your own post-office box. It grows with you as you navigate through your career. I have some convincing to do: according to recent surveys "only seven percent of the general population" has a personal website (Bianchi, 2014).

If you are seeking employment, you definitely should have a personal website. I think of it as a multidimensional resume in the sense that you provide layers of content that not only explain and describe your skills and capabilities but also demonstrates them. Being able to demonstrate with a personal website is a huge advantage over a traditional resume or social-media profile. If you have the time, writing a blog convinces others that you have your own insights. I conducted a survey of recruiters and presented the results in *A Skills-Based Approach to Developing a Career*. A large majority of the respondents are more than willing to review a personal website and the various forms of media you publish on it. You might as well give them what they want to see.

In the long-term, use a personal website to establish your online personal brand. Keep it throughout your career, all the way from college to late career. Repurpose the content of the personal website based on what you are trying to accomplish with your career. If you are looking for employment, it replaces a resume. If you are employed, it is an opportunity for your ecosystem to learn more about you on a deeper level. And of course, passive employment seeking is becoming far more common. A recruiter visits your website and may offer you a better, more long-term position. Finally, later in your career, it is a platform for you to share your credentials and validate skills.

Paul Angone shares the sentiment that a personal website acts as the centerpiece of an online personal brand. In *101 Secrets For Your Twenties*, he says: "Creating your own website is the #1 biggest, baddest, and boldest amplifier of all job searching, platform building, brand bolstering efforts" (Angone, 2013).

Here are some key points:

- While seeking employment, you want to make sure there is enough content on your personal website for a potential employer to make a decision on hiring you; it essentially replaces the resume. It is a multidimensional resume—something that takes advantage of media, interactivity, and communication features of the Internet.
- Job seeking is a series of finite games you compete in until you find employment. The content of a personal website is tailored for an employment evaluation. You target a job by sending a personalized e-mail invitation; advertising on Twitter, Google+, or Facebook; or responding to a job board and providing a link back to your personal website.
- Establishing a personal brand is an infinite game where you differentiate from others to become *that* guy—the graphic designer, social-media expert, or finance guru. You are competing with other professionals in your target market for the same title. The content of the personal website changes as its primary focus becomes perception; you want to demonstrate that you are an expert in your profession (with samples of work) and have fresh insight (with a blog). A good personal website platform makes this transition from job seeker to brander seamless.
- You will go through a cycle of job seeking and personal branding throughout your career. You will most likely change careers a few times, so you need a personal website that changes with you. Think of your personal website as a repository of all your professional content you have collected over the years—a database and a catalogue of files.
- Actively seeking employment is like casting and reeling a fish in right away; you cast as many times as possible to increase your chances of catching a fish (or a job

offer). Passively seeking employment is casting a line rigged with a bobber, so once you cast, it becomes a waiting game, and you can go off and do other things. When the bobber sinks, you know there is a fish biting the line (a job offer).
- You can establish consistency by getting everyone to a personal website. If all roads lead to your personal website, you have more control over the perception of your target audience. So link to your personal website in your social-media profiles.
- Learn about the effectiveness of your online personal brand by monitoring the traffic results to your personal website in Google Analytics. When you launch your personal website, make sure you create a Google Analytics account and install the script on each of the pages of your personal website. You can then view: number of unique visitors, where the visitors came from (i.e. Google or Bing search or a referral), keywords they searched on to get to your page, the length of time spent on your website, what links that were clicked on, and much more.

Personal Website
Something that adapts to the changes in your life.

Seeking College Graduate School Acceptance
Demonstrate core transferable skills with video and blog.

Actively Seeking Employment
Expand content so viewing a resume is not required. Present & validate skills.

Personal Branding
Show personality. Prove credibility. Establish identity. Differentiate.

Passively Seeking Employment
Use SEO. Coordinate pull approach. Present & validate skills.

How to Build an Online Personal Brand

I have discussed the key elements of an online personal brand, so you might be wondering if there is a method or an approach to establish your own. By now I have hopefully convinced you to invest in one, so if you decide to start today, where do you begin? Below is a basic framework. I talk about themes, so if you want to get more detailed instructions from a practitioner, I suggest checking out some of the books I mention in the appendix.

The first step is to get a basic conception of disciplines or subjects that interest you. This does not have to be exact right now, but being self-aware is an important foundation of your personal brand. Think about a value proposition: how are you a solution to a problem. I strongly suggest taking Gallup's StrengthFinder test to identify your core-competencies, which are presented on both a functional and emotional level. Concentrating on what you do best is an inspiring, uplifting way to start your journey.

Second, take an inventory of your brand assets and liabilities. Start with your assets so you are in a positive frame of mind. Tag your most valuable pieces of intellectual property so you can maintain copyright privileges and accentuate them on your personal website and then link to them in social media. Think about coursework – papers and presentations, content you created related to hobbies and personal experiences, and/or any work products that you own. For successful projects that you do not own copyright privileges (likely if it is something you worked for an employer), find ways to talk about your contribution and identify references to back you up. You might even ask your employer for rights to share a snip-it of the work product on your personal website. Finally, think about ideas and insights in your pipeline- stuff you plan to work on later. Assets are the substance behind your brand.

Third, identify your target market. Think about various channels you are trying to reach: clients, partners, associates, mentors, and classmates. Appropriate targeting is critical in the early stages because it keeps you grounded, so you can calibrate the process of making connections and publishing content. This establishes clear boundaries for your branding efforts – you cannot reach everyone.

Fourth, identify the competition. There is someone else who has already established a personal brand similar to yours so you want to benchmark; take an introspective look at what they are doing right and wrong (Celeste, 2014). You also have to differentiate from close competitors, so find ways to leverage your unique skills to standout from them. This is an assessment of where you stand and need to go with your brand.

Fifth, build your personal website. Buy a domain name that is your real name and/or a slogan and then start constructing your website. In the early stages of branding, the primary objective of your personal website depends on where you are in your career and what you are trying to accomplish. It might be used to increase your chances in landing favorable employment, so in this case, make sure it has enough content so an employer makes an employment evaluation. Otherwise, consider it a platform to project your personal brand. Regardless, the ultimate purpose is to establish your professional identity – something you can claim ownership of and keep throughout your career.

Sixth, start building profiles in each of the big four social media services: Twitter, Google+, Facebook, and LinkedIn. With all of the profiles, you want to create and publish an effective, personal background image (for consistency, it could be the same image). In all of the profiles, with the exception of Twitter, you want to publish your skill set in its entirety. Skill sets make you accessible so you *get found* by your target audience. As you develop the individual profiles, consider the following:

- With Twitter, use your elevator pitch, start following key hashtags in your subject of interest, and identify key influencers.
- With Facebook, you probably already have a well-established presence – so the idea is to begin a conversion process. Evaluate your profile and Facebook wall and make sure there is nothing that could be misconstrued if taken in a professional context.
- With LinkedIn, you must create an effective resume and post a sharp facial profile. Presenting and validating your skill set is critical because of the search engine Recruiter and the skill endorsement interface.

- With Google+, your profile should have an effective tag line. Like with Twitter, connect with thought leaders. Start thinking about what circles (sub-networks) you might want to join or create.

Seventh, curate your own content. Think about creating a blog, Tweeting thoughts, creating video and graphics (which you may or may not publish in Pinterest or YouTube), and/or writing articles (which you may publish in Scribd). The experts say you should have your own blog and regularly Tweet, but I think it depends on your profession and passion. Yet, I still think you should create your own content because it is physically easy to do (meaning you can create files on a computer or mobile device), moreover, it ensures you generate insights. You force yourself to reflect and think on subjects that interest you.

Eighth, get feedback. Label your online personal brand as being in an 'Alpha' stage, and start releasing it to your small, trustworthy cadre. Try to get a handle on if you are being perceived as you intend on being perceived; understanding perceptions is tricky. This is an ongoing procedure, though I think an initial query should be completed before amplifying your presence in social media.

Ninth, make connections in social media but start slow. Coming back to employing *a bottom up approach*, you need to firmly establish your identity and then project it onto networks. If you think about the social dynamics in making connections, then you realize that you can wait; in most cases it does not matter if you connect with someone now or in a week. Sure there is the exception of those professionals who gain influence because of thousands of connections, but for most of us, it does not really matter. Regarding connections, think quality trumps quantity. Connections play an important role in your personal brand.

Tenth, evolve and update accordingly. You are making a career long commitment, so you are going to have to make changes regularly (perhaps even on a weekly basis). The development of a skill set – the functional element – is an ongoing requirement. You are always building and validating skills, so to establish credibility, you must present the latest developments regarding your skill set.

Eleventh, behave according to the expectations laid out in your personal brand – be authentic. For example, if you are a *thought leader*, you commit to a regiment of blogging once a week and Tweeting daily.

Finally, keep abreast of the latest technologies and applications and respond accordingly. The scope and norms related to online personal branding are always changing. For example, using LinkedIn to make professional connections has become a norm (only three years ago it was not a norm). Regarding scope, we are being inundated with mobile applications. Now, younger professionals must have a mobile presence. I think the notion of a personal website becomes a norm in the near future; most people will have one and it becomes the new employment evaluation platform – effectively replacing the resume.

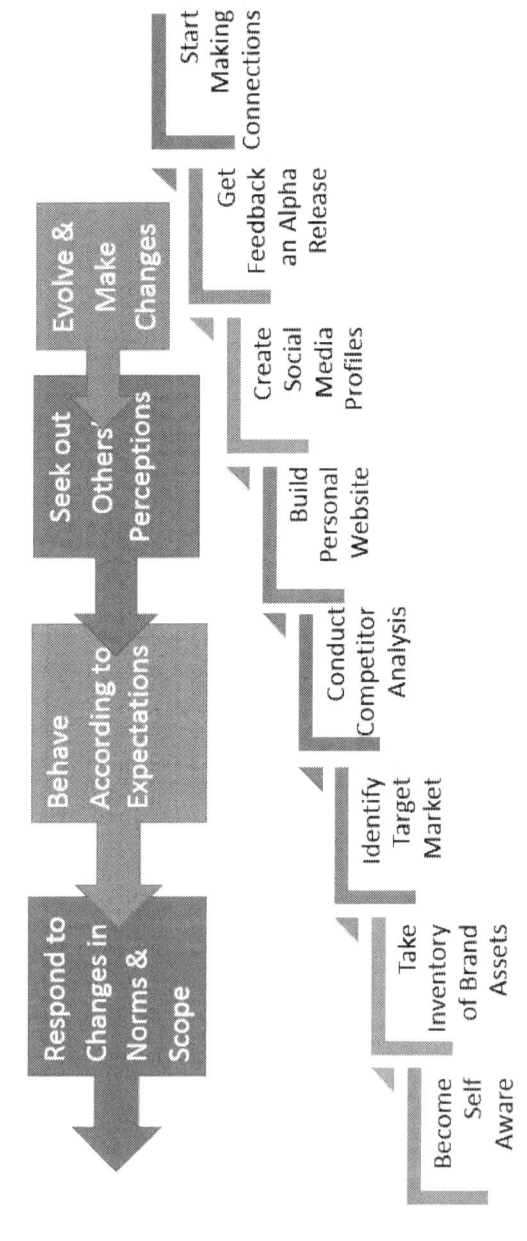

Employment Evaluations

Ideally you want to be considered for employment opportunities based on an online personal brand rather than a summary of your qualifications and your education and employment experiences—a traditional resume. Why? Because you can create a holistic impression of yourself, where you have control over a potential employer's experience as he or she considers hiring you. You have an opportunity to communicate to a reviewer through various forms of media: video, graphics, and text. In addition, you can convince someone of your skills and knowledge by providing work samples, insights in a blog, ingenuity in a video, and social savvy in social media. Incorporate motivational fit into your content so that you maximize your influence. Finally, you can infuse personality, style, and culture into your brand—something that is not tolerated in a strictly formatted MS Word resume.

The expectations of employers and recruiters are moving toward an online personal brand. Most employers are reviewing your digital footprint by Googling your name and viewing the results, typically a combination of social-media profiles, background information, and a personal website. Obviously the extent to which employers review your online presence varies largely on what type of profession you are in. Marketers, IT professionals, and leaders should expect a fairly extensive review, while doctors, accountants, and bankers might expect a quick one. Although some of these professions favoring prevention content will have more of an online presence because they are accountable. For example, a doctor will have to make his credentials transparent to his or her patients, especially as doctors are required to continue building their skills throughout their career.

As more and more professions adopt new technologies, job seekers will have to demonstrate their proficiencies. The easiest way to do so is by providing an example where you have utilized a particular technology. Teaching comes to mind. Teachers are expected to use technologies in their classroom, and with this comes a lot of responsibility. It is necessary for teachers to show they understand the implications of the technologies they are employing. This is why I think teachers are going to benefit from having an online presence (even though many say it is unnecessary).

With so many online learning channels, like MOOCs, professionals need to be able to share their experiences ad hoc. One professional gets a traditional college degree while another professional takes a collection of online courses. A standard resume does not work well. On the other hand, a personal website has the flexibility to present various education backgrounds. Moreover, it is possible to provide examples of what your learned.

Credibility, an important element of a personal brand, can be accomplished in various ways. Mozilla recently released a powerful online badging system, where professionals can earn a badge verifying a proficiency in just about anything. It is difficult to establish credibility with a standard resume, both in describing your competency and in verifying you are legit. (There are always cases of resume fraud.) But, by incorporating badges into the fabric of a personal website or LinkedIn profile, you have a secure mechanism to prove you are what you say you are. Your skill set can be effectively validated.

It is possible for your entire professional network to back you in an employment evaluation. An employer simply visits your LinkedIn profile to see who is endorsing your skills. They can then follow through and connect with those who endorsed you to learn more about the connections' experiences with you. This is dramatically more effective than having a list of three seasoned references talking on your behalf. So the identity aspect of your personal brand now has weight in an employment evaluation, and this is a positive thing.

Finally, the aura element of a personal brand should be an important part of an employment evaluation. (Again, this is almost impossible to capture in a resume.) For better or worse, you want to help employers to get to know your personality, strengths, and values. Are you a learner? Are you a speaker? Are you compassionate? Consider taking the Gallup Strength Finder test to identify your top five strengths. Gallup says you dramatically improve performance if you and the people you interact with leverage these top strengths. So you should find a way to tell an employer about these five strengths.

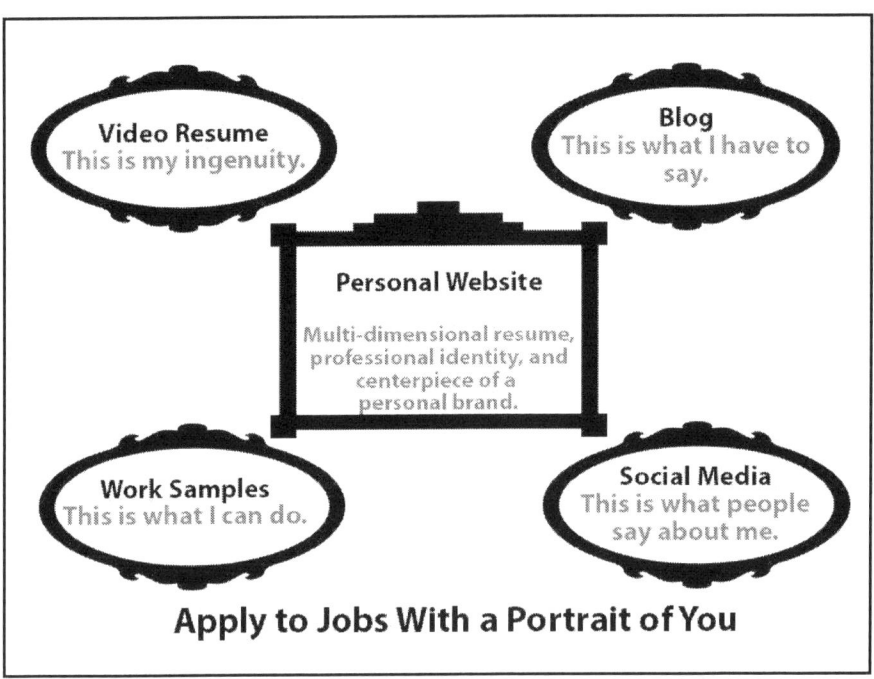

Leadership: Personal Branding

With the majority of personal branding books, the authors write to an audience of leaders. There is a strong connation between leadership and personal branding. In this book, I share my model that I hope is applicable to all professionals. I also make the argument that all professionals should participate in it. Nevertheless, if you are a leader, the value of a personal brand is magnified for two big reasons. First, you are expected to inspire and motive a team – coworkers, partners, and clients. An effective online personal brand installs confidence in your team and gives them the opportunity to be a part of your mission (definition of your being) and vision (definition of what you are becoming) (Rampersad, 2009, p. 33). A leader must vocalize their vision. Second, as I mention in a later chapter, a leader's personal brand must coincide with the company brand; both have to be in synch. In many situations, a leader's brand is accessible (sometimes idolized) by the general public.

If you think of big IT companies, for many of them, you are familiar with the personal brands of their leaders. It is about not only their position and credentials, but also their interests and values. Let's take the example of Mark Zuckerberg. Off of the top of my mind, here are some elements I identify with. He has a boyish, laidback charm but is wickedly smart. He loves talking technology and social connectedness, still participates in coding software (even when it could be considered beneath him), and donates to educational causes. A picture of him etched in my mind is him wearing a hoody to Facebook's IPO on Wall Street. There are many other examples: Steve Jobs (Apple), Bill Gates (Microsoft), Marissa Mayer (Yahoo), Richard Branson (Virgin Group), Jeff Weiner (LinkedIn), and Sergey Brin (Google).

Of course, I have to use examples of leaders of larger, successful companies to illustrate my point that a company is represented by the personal brand of their leader. However, I think it is applicable to leaders of most companies. There is a convergence of personal and company brands in communications, especially in social media. If you are interested in learning more about a leader, then follow them in Twitter, connect with them in Google+, like their Facebook page, and/or read insights in their LinkedIn posts. You can also search on their name in Google or Bing. They probably have a personal website and information about them on company pages.

A leader's personal website has all of the same characteristics I talked about earlier with the addition of needing to inspire a team. You should establish credibility, so your team knows how and why you are the leader. Let your team review your educational and professional experiences and demonstrate your skills and knowledge. Help your team get to know you on a personal level so they are comfortable around you. Share aspects of your vision with them. A blog is an excellent way to help your team understand your thoughts.

Showing vision is paramount for leaders. Here are a few points regarding sharing vision:

- **Returns take time.** Actualizing a vision often takes many, many years.
- **Stick to your guns.** Standby the core principles of your vision. You might have to change course and adapt to other perspectives regarding some of them. However, conviction is a requirement in fending off competitors and naysayers.
- **Buttress your vision.** It takes additional time to obtain auxiliary support mechanisms like a book, but it is

worth the investment for two reasons. First, it establishes credibility. You may have critics who are smarter, more ambitious than you, so winning them over requires proof. Second, it provides some intellectual property protection.

- **Every idea and concept matters in communicating your vision.**
- **Always voice your vision.** Having a vision is respectable and contagious so don't be afraid in spreading the word.
- **Rally the troops behind the vision.** Ultimately, it is powerful having a team in synch with your vision where they speak, teach, and breathe it.

Leaders motivate and inspire their team by showing vision. As a leader navigates through their career, it is often their vision that endures. A leader's skill set is important to establish credibility, but often their aura and identity element come more into play. Charisma and connectedness are critical in being an effective leader.

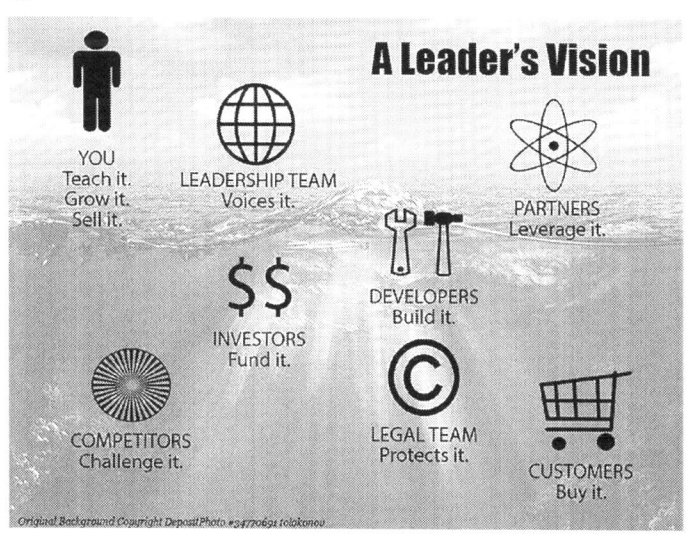

Millennials

Marketers, technologists, educationalists, politicians, and many others are trying to define the much hyped millennial generation. Some of their generalizations say that millennials are digital natives, religiously unaffiliated, self-centered (perhaps by necessity), supportive of social-welfare issues, better educated, demographically diverse, unmarried (and likely living with parents), and optimistic of their future. Millennials are defined as being born from the early 1980s to the early 2000s.

I decided to include a chapter on the millennial generation because it is clear members of this generation must develop online personal brands, and they also represent a large number of the workforce — 36 percent of it (Schawbel, Promote Yourself: The New Rules For Career Success, 2013). Millennials are already experienced in social media and developing a persona, and now they must transform this persona into something cohesive.

The sooner a person gets it (that they need an online personal brand), the faster they can start building one. A strong online personal brand — reflected in a personal website — can be effective as early as college admissions. Hopefully, getting high school students to think about long-term reflections of themselves helps them make smart decisions regarding a college education and/or job training and then perform with vigor. Rather than showing up to college campuses academically adrift (Arum & Roksa, 2011).

Millennials are digital natives, meaning they were raised with the prevalence of computers and devices, social media, video games, apps, and the Internet. Eighty-one percent are on Facebook and have a median of 250 friends. Technology has a major influence on education for a few reasons: online learning platforms make personalized and adaptive learning a reality, information is easily accessible to all, and discussion forums make feedback and social learning possible.

Millennials and future generations must continually learn throughout their careers. Previously, professionals went to college for two to four years, earned a degree, and then went to work. Now, because of the rapid adoption of technology and how fast information flows, you cannot rest on your laurels. You have to constantly tune your skills and build knowledge. Perhaps take at least one course throughout your career. Stay on top of what the latest influencers are saying in your field through active participation in social media and blogs. With an online personal brand, make your lifelong learning process transparent by presenting degrees, online courses, certifications, job training, and other experiences on a personal website. It shows commitment, passion, and vision.

Despite being saddled with more student-loan debt than any other previous generation and having little assurance social security will be there when they retire, millennials are notably more optimistic than other generations. A whopping eighty-five percent say they are earning enough now or will in the future. (Significantly higher than any of the other generations.) Many from past generations paid off student loans within a few years after graduating (the ratio of debt to annual salary was much lower, and the cost of living was lower), so it was never really an issue. However, millennials are confronted with lifelong debt. Where does the optimism come from?

Millennials have a deterministic attitude that if they work hard, things will turn out OK regardless of a poor economy or few job prospects. In *The Next America*, Paul Taylor calls millennials the most "stubborn optimists" (Taylor, 2014). Millennials realize college debt is inevitable, so why stress out about it?

An online personal brand has significance because it is what connects a collection of education and employment experiences into something cohesive. If you take on a stepping-stone job, you can usually find ways to make relevant points regarding your career goals. If you have been unemployed for a period of time, you can still build skills and knowledge, write on blogs or social media, and network. These are all visible affirmations that you were investing in your career while you were unemployed. The bottom line is that, if you produce compelling, insightful work, it does not matter if an employer is paying you for it. And getting certified proves you have necessary skills and usually commands the same respect as if you did the work.

> **Millennials**
>
> Information at Their Fingerprints • Personal Branders • Google • Wikipedia • Quora • Self guided learners • Mozilla Badges • Khan Academy • YouTube • MOOCs • Born after 1980 • 97% own a computer, 94% own a cell phone • Self Promotion • Online Identity • Personal Content • Professional Content • New Age Skills • Thirty-six percent of workforce • Computational Thinking • Virtual Collaboration • New Media Literacy • Design Mindset • Educated • Informed • Tech Savvy • Community Minded • Think 'Global Impact' • Connected to Parents • Communicate Instantly • Multi-taskers • Seek societal purpose with employers • Individualistic • Work from home or office • Facebook • Google+ • Twitter • Seek Responsibility • Happiness is a job requirement

Here are some characteristics of millennials:

- Millennials are informed. With Twitter, they receive a blitz of ideas. With LinkedIn, they connect to their own professional ecosystem. They can subscribe to whatever blog, website, or online community interests them.
- Millennials know the latest devices and applications. At all stages of education, students are using tablets,

laptops, and/or smartphones. I took a MOOC on Emerging Technologies in K–12 and learned that students are using all of these devices, social media, and online courses and games.
- Millennials are looking for happiness and meaning, not just financial gain (Smith & Aaker, 2013). Millennials seek purpose and want to thrive in what they do every day. It is no surprise the best places to work are at companies where employees feel what they do has a global impact.
- Millennials are community-minded. Ninety-two percent of millennials believe businesses should be measured by not only profit but also societal purpose. Many are willing to do pro bono work. For example, Advisory Board (a DC company) got 98 percent of its staff to commit to community service so far this year — something they claim attracts and retains millennials (Halzack, 2013).
- Millennials face a challenging job market. According to one study, the employment rate dropped from 84 to 72 percent for adults aged twenty-one to twenty-five during 2000 and 2012 (Porter, 2013). Part of the problem is a skills gap — employers have a difficult time hiring new employees because they lack the necessary technical skills. To close the gap, millennials must stay abreast of the latest technologies and applications.

Millennial Survey

In late 2013 to early 2014, I conducted a survey to understand what millennials think about online personal branding. I targeted this segment of the population because it is the first generation that must invest in one (as I said in the last chapter). In addition, millennials already have an online presence so they will have to make a transition when they become professionals. How are they going to manage all the personal content from their teenage and college years? What about the hundreds of connections they have made? And at some point, they will face maturity.

Most of the respondents feel an online personal brand is somewhat important, and only ten percent think it is essential. A large number, twenty-seven percent, think it is not important. I am not surprised that such a large number of respondents say it is not important. They probably do not know much about it. I used a broad sample canvassing many professional backgrounds, and unfortunately, most articles and books about personal branding cater to white-collar professionals.

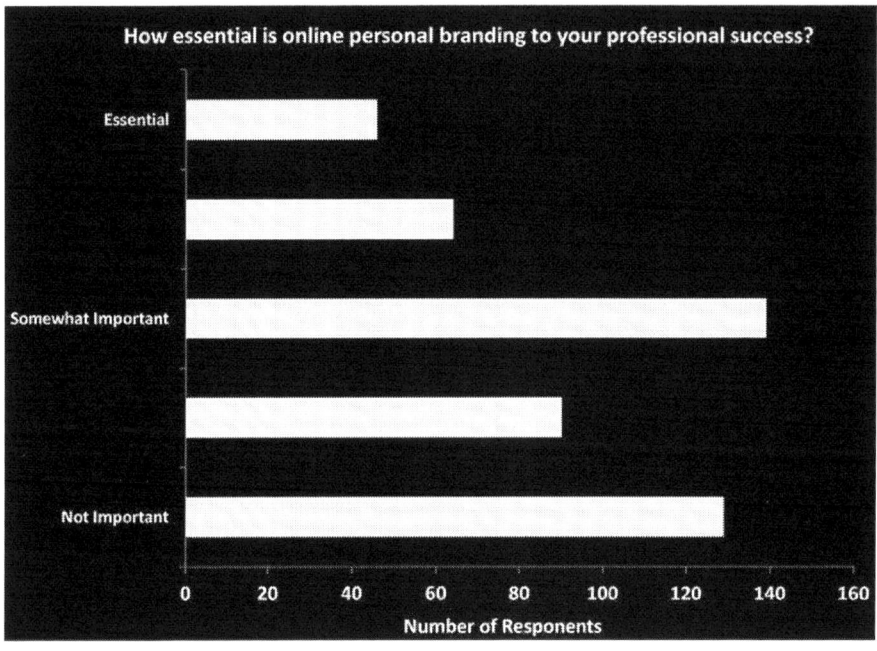

In the survey, I asked what millennials thought about having a personal website. The response to the statement "I should have a personal website" was largely split between agreeing and disagreeing. The largest two segments were thirty-two percent saying maybe and thirty-one percent saying they disagree. Most of the respondents (seventy-one percent) were not sure having a personal website is worth the expense, while forty-one percent thought it was too much self-promotion. A large chunk of the respondents (sixty-five percent) want a personal website for free, and twenty-four percent would pay five to ten dollars a month. (Millennials are well acquainted to getting their web service and apps for free.)

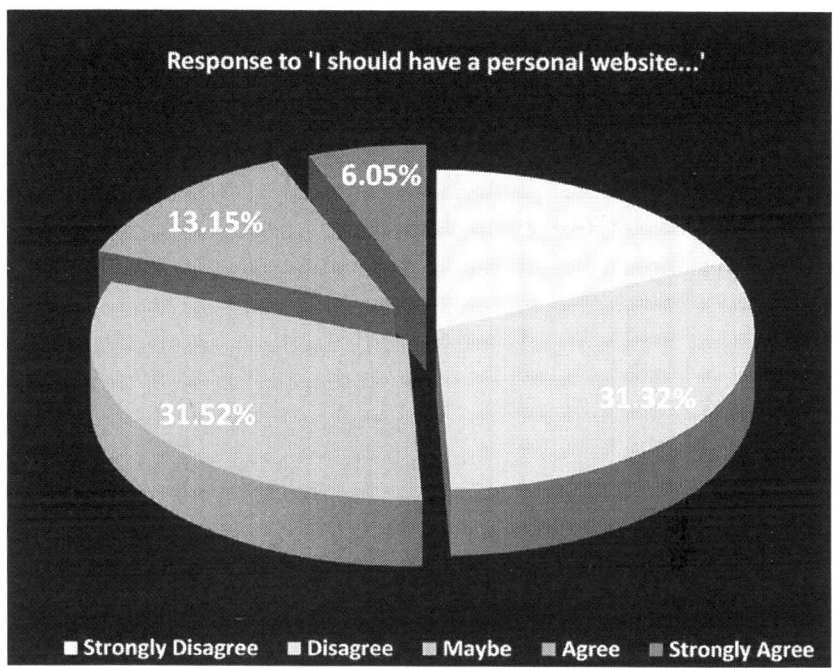

Some conclusions based on the results of the survey:

- Millennials are not all onboard to invest in their future by developing an online personal brand, yet they really should because of their digital footprint—something all future employers are going to review. (I find it unfortunate that so many of the personal-branding books are written for the elite—people studying at Ivy League schools or targeting Google or Microsoft as an employer.)
- In open-ended responses, millennials equate the need for an online personal brand to their future career path or as a replacement to a resume. For example, some respondents said they are going into teaching, so branding is unnecessary. I argue most professions do or will require an online presence. So teachers establish a repertoire with parents online, and online learning is replacing the traditional classroom. Personal branding is much, much deeper than a single-dimensional resume.

- A personal website should be the centerpiece of a personal brand. Millennials are not convinced in the necessity in having a personal website, demonstrated by a separate survey saying only fifteen percent of them have one (Bianchi, 2014). They think having a personal website as more of a hassle and want one for free. What they are not seeing is that a personal website nails down an identity, with a domain name, and establishes ownership of content. Both of these are critical because of the ever expanding reach of social media and networks. It is worth paying for something when you own it.
- Millennials relate having a personal website with self-promotion. Of course, there is a lot of promotion in putting together a good personal website. However, for many professions, it also involves prevention—validating your skills and credibility.

A Personal Brand and a Company Brand

I would like to discuss how your personal brand may coincide or collide with your employer's company brand and what you should do about it.

I started to think about how promoting a company brand might impact promoting your personal brand after reading Gregg Ledermann's book *Brand Integrity*. Ledermann suggests that leaders define and then rally their employers around a company brand (Lederman, 2007). What I think separates Ledermann's viewpoint from others' is the deep level of engagement of employees. They are expected to behave according to a company brand. It is not simply reciting a mission statement or logo but acting, thinking, and speaking in a way that promotes the company brand. How does behaving according to your company brand affect your personal brand?

When your personal brand coincides with a company brand, then it seems everything works out well. This is the case if you are a leader, or perhaps, a marketer in the company; you probably defined the company brand. Otherwise, you probably buy into aspects of a company brand but necessary all of them, yet you still have to behave accordingly. A simple example is a dress code. You may have to wear a suit and be clean-shaven when you go to work, but you prefer shorts and a goatee. There are those of us who think a dress code makes a strong impact on work performance, and there are those of us whose primary concern is being unique or comfortable. It is the same when you take things online.

Many of us would like for our online personal brand to be based on our self-expression, but boundaries based on an employer's company brand might exist. You might not be able to have your website appear a certain way (analogous to the dress-code example), and the content should have similar motivational fit. If your employer takes on a heavy prevention approach to the company brand, then it would be difficult to pull off a heavy promotion approach with your personal brand. This might seem heavy-handed, but employers have access to your digital footprint and can reserve the right to terminate your employment based on what they find. Sometime this makes sense, especially in a small technology company. They cannot afford miscommunications related to their company brand because of how you represent yourself online. Crossed lines regarding personal and company branding should be worked out during the hiring process for the benefit of all parties. It makes sense that "thirty-nine percent of employers dig into candidates on social sites" - forty-three percent of the time finding something to decide against hiring them (Weber, 2014). If there is a problem later on, it is likely an employer will ask you to make changes to fall in line with their company brand.

It gets tricky when you are an early-career professional working at a stepping-stone job. You are only planning to be at a company for a couple years but are expected to behave according to expectations. This is where you have to be mindful of your long-term plan or vision. In the short-term, you are building skills and knowledge and making connections, and this should be your primary concern in a stepping-stone job—it is what you will take to your next job. Much of skill building it repetition, which is necessary to master new knowledge and skills (Churchill, 2011, p. 20). It is unlikely that you agree to all of the expected behaviors of your employer, so you will have to conform to elements of the company brand. It happens offline, so expect for it to happen online. Scott Monty, a social media expert at Ford Motors says: "If you are employed by a notable brand, it should always be brand first, self second" (Glaser, 2009).

The interviewing process and (if you are hired) the onboard process is a great time to understand how your personal brand fits with a company brand. In fact, as you are courted by potential employers, you should be interviewing them. You want to see if they follow your core values so you can estimate how happy you might be working there. Is the general office vibe laid-back or strict? Do coworkers naturally congregate and socialize? Is loyalty valued more than creativity? After you are hired and accept the offer, the first weeks—the job training—are a crucial time for you and your employer. It is your time to seed relationships with the people you will be interacting with on an everyday basis, get orientated with the projects you will be working on, and familiarize with the company culture.

Hiring you is a big investment by your employer, so it behooves them to provide you with an adequate onboard process. According to an article published by Wynhurst Group, "New employees are 58 percent more likely to stay with a company for at least three years if they experience a structured orientation program" (Farren, 2014).

Younger professionals are looking to companies that are with the times. An IT professional is looking for a company that is adopting the newest technologies, using the latest project management, and offering some part of the company's value. The rigid vertical structure is replaced by a horizontal structure, and there is an opportunity to invest in the future of the company. The ideas and reflection of individuals is more important than conformity; personal branding is promoted. Being creative trumps loyalty. It is better to get the ideas out than to never hear them at all. A horizontal company structure, individualism, and creativity are all aspects of a company brand that are common among new, upcoming organizations (Aruda & Dixson, Career Distinction: Stand Out By Building Your Brand, 2007).

Professionals might be labeled as 'organization-lovers' or 'free agents'. Organization lovers are willing to put in extra effort for the success of the company and are team players. They of course buy into the company brand. Free agents are more invested in their own success and are self-directed. They buy into their personal brand. There are 'pros' and 'cons' for a company with each mindset (Shellenbarger, 2014).

Some large companies are investing in their employees by providing them with workshops and training on personal branding as part of their career development (Aruda & Dixson, Career Distinction: Stand Out By Building Your Brand, 2007). They understand that a powerful personal brand reflects well on their company brand, employees are happier when they know their company invests in their well-being.

There is still opportunity to express aspects of an online personal brand that do not relate to or distract from an employer's company brand. This will almost always be the case if you are underemployed (working a job that you are overqualified for) and might be relevant if you plan to make a move to another career. Perhaps your current job just pays the bills. In any case, you can start working on your online personal brand for a future career. Some of things you can do proactively include blogging to share your insights, joining online communities with influencers in a career field, and building and validating required skills and then presenting them on a personal website and LinkedIn, Facebook, and Google+ profiles. Become a curator of your personal website. Think of it as something you carry on with you as you make necessary transitions in your career.

Of course, whenever possible, you want to anticipate a career move because it gives you an advantage to make connections and position yourself to take on a new role. With the competitive nature of attracting talent, employers are always looking to snatch up their competitor's talent, and with LinkedIn, these acquisitions are ever more visible. Think about how many of your connections have changed employers in the past few months. And this leads into the idea of passively seeking employment where you utilize a pull approach to attract potential suitors. Instead of actively applying to more satiable careers, dangle your online personal brand out there, and let recruiters and potential employers find you.

If you are currently employed, understand your employer's company brand and how it fits with your personal brand. When you start a job, learn about your employer's expectations, and determine if there are any major conflicts. For example, if you already tweet on subjects related to your job, ask your employer if they have any rules against such behavior. Once boundaries are established, find ways to leverage your current professional experience into the fabric of your personal brand. Always move forward with your long-term vision and never lose sight of long-term goals. Finally, think of your online personal brand as eye candy for recruiters and potential employers.

Another perspective is to have a primary career (the main source of income) and work towards a second career (a second source of income and perhaps a passionate pursuit). This is what Mariam Salpeter and Hanna Morgan describe with the acronym MOXIE (managing other x-tra income engagements) and suggest having because of the challenge in finding and keeping stable employment while being satisfied (Salpeter & Morgan, 2013). Because it is hard to find work, many of us are forced to take a job because we have the skills for it even though it is not something we like doing. So a second career might give you that sense of fulfillment. It also might be something you plan to do full-time later in your career if it makes financial sense. Developing a personal brand helps you move forward with your second career.

Build your personal website, and start seeding connections in social media around a second career. Find ways to build the skills you will need, and present and validate them whenever you can. Use social media to establish credibility. You might get on Twitter every night and write and respond to a few tweets. Likewise, establish connections, join groups, and read articles on LinkedIn and Facebook as well. It could take an hour a night, but if you stick to the regimen, it can have a huge payoff: connections and credibility (both of which you will need to launch a second career). Clearly this type of commitment is manageable if you work a day job and keep up other responsibilities.

Constructing your online personal brand based on a second career is invigorating. It allows you to take control, use self-expression, and be your own boss. You take on a long-term strategy that does not rely on a bumpy ride typical with full-time employment gigs. For many, a second career injects engagement that a day job does not accomplish. Finally, it is something that motivates you with a sense of purpose — something you work toward your entire career. That is powerful. You are always building and validating necessary skills and moving toward becoming an expert. I agree with Mariam Salpeter and Hanna Morgan that second careers will become increasingly more common. I also bet more professionals associate their true online personal brand with their second career.

And another perspective is that a company's brand is actually the combination of its employees' personal brands. Think about the visibility of the leadership team with a technology start-up; simply click on their bios on the company website or view their profiles on LinkedIn. In *Ditch Dare Do*, the authors summarize this perspective: "Today, the individuals working in the company are the authentic face of the brand, not the reverse. Employees' brands and their company's brand are inextricably linked" (Arruda & Dib, 2013, p. 4).

Maturation Process of a Personal Brand

Professionals go through a maturation process throughout their career. I think the process starts in high school as students are forced to start choosing classes (APs and/or in STEM fields) and considering their next move. But for most, the awakening, when someone truly understands their professional calling does not happen until their late twenties to early thirties. This is part of the reason the average professional goes through so many job and career changes in their lifetime. Yet personal branding is still important for early career professionals. In fact, I believe the earlier professionals take command of it, the faster they find career happiness and fulfillment. Moreover, conceptualizing a personal brand helps professionals avoid making catastrophic career mistakes.

Most highschoolers have little insight about their career goals. According to Richard Arum and Josipa Roksa, "Only about one in five young people in the 12 – 22 year age range express a clear vision of where they want to go, what they want to accomplish in life, and why" (Arum & Roksa, 2011). This is not surprising. Much of their education is based on learning reading, writing, and math skills so there is a lack of exposure to technical skills and career responsibilities. However, I believe this is changing because of access to online learning platforms, social media communication, and career information published online. Anyone can take an introductory online course to feel out a discipline. Anyone can create a social media account and follow thought leaders in a discipline. And, like with anything else, there is an abundance of information online regarding career guidance.

In addition, there are many online resources that help late-teenagers become more self-aware and provide career guidance. (I have tried web services provided by MyPlan and Kuder.) I recommend that all college bound students take a personality, interests, and/or strengths test because self-knowledge prepares them to make two impactful decisions: choosing a college and then a major. Both hold significant weight on later career possibilities. One college president refers to the period as a "college's ten-year 'zone of impact', which includes the year before college, the four years of undergraduate studies, and five years after college" (Selingo, 2013). Related to online personal branding, I think highschoolers should have a personal website that supplements their college application. Showing vision at this stage gives them a leg up in the college admissions process.

Eighty percent of high school graduates will enter higher education at some point (Bok, 2013, p. 77). This is where they build skills and knowledge needed for a career, become civic minded, and have a social experience. There are a few advantages in thinking about online personal branding at this stage in a career. First, students think on a course level (as opposed to a degree level). So they make sure each course counts, whether it is job-related or the subject interests them. They should publish what courses they took along with samples of coursework in their LinkedIn profile and personal website. Second, students think about establishing professional identities and start making connections. Professors make excellent references and mentors, and steer students in positive directions. Classmates become the foundation of a professional network for years to come. Finally, students have a better perspective of their fields of interest so they can start the process of differentiating their own personal brands.

After a stint of higher education (where six of ten students enrolled in a bachelor's degree graduate with one (National Center for Education Statistics)), most early career professionals seek employment as soon as possible so they are able to pay their living expenses and student loans. The lucky ones get employed in a field that fits nicely with their career path, while the rest get whatever is available and often end up underemployed – doing work below a skill level. Regardless, it is an exploration process where young professionals hone their skills and identify core-competencies, passions, and values – based on professional experiences and self-reflection (as opposed to educational experiences and parents' directives).

Early career professionals also have the difficult task of converting a hefty load of personal content and connections into an online personal brand. This is a daunting, unfamiliar task. No other generation has gone through this process, because the notion of an online presence was non-existent. They must rummage through their content published in social media and remove anything that could damage their reputation. They must cycle through connections and consider dropping ones that leave obnoxious posts that appear on their Facebook wall.

For early career professionals, it is important to string together experiences that emphasize their personal brand. They are most likely only at the starting gate so want to find ways to show career direction by building and validating the skills they need for their future. Early career professionals should also keep getting more self-aware. In his book 12 Steps to Freedom, Paul Rega introduces his Intuitive Personal Assessment: "(IPA) is a concept I have developed that simply states: because of who we are, dictated by a combination of life experiences, genetics and environmental forces, between the ages of 25-30, we intuitively know and are aware of what our true career path shall be" (Rega, 2013).

Personal branding for mid-career professionals is exciting if they are on the right career. They have an established connection base, expertise with their skill set, and confidence in their communications. They have an identity established on a personal website and in social media, where they share insights and contribute in discussions. It is a time to validate their skills. They know how they want to be perceived on an emotional level, and are hopefully successful in getting their audience to perceive them that way. This is when a professional is ready to project it.

This mid-career stage is harder for professionals who are not on the right career. It is more difficult to make a major career transitions because of family and financial obligations. For example, a banker with a wife and two kids cannot easily go back to college to get a teaching degree. Career pivots are still common because workers are bound to projects rather than companies. Rebranding is possible but challenging. Professionals have to go through the process of establishing credibility with new skills and domain knowledge all over again. And it might seem awkward because of the nature of online connections and content. They will have to make decisions regarding what to keep and what to lose. Another option for a restless mid-career professional is to develop a personal brand based on a second career, perhaps moonlighting in a profession he or she is passionate about and would do fulltime if it brought in enough money.

Late career professionals are usually at the top of the career chain, having validated their skills and established an effective personal brand. In many fields, they are the leaders or mentors of the next generation. For some late career professionals, their essence is about sharing wisdom. For others, their essence is about giving back or following a passion so they pursue a completely different career, something less stressful and with purpose. As a semiretirement career expert says, "It's so much more about reconfiguring, taking the old and blending it with the new and coming up with something that's going to excite you in the second half of the third quarter" (Ellin, 2014).

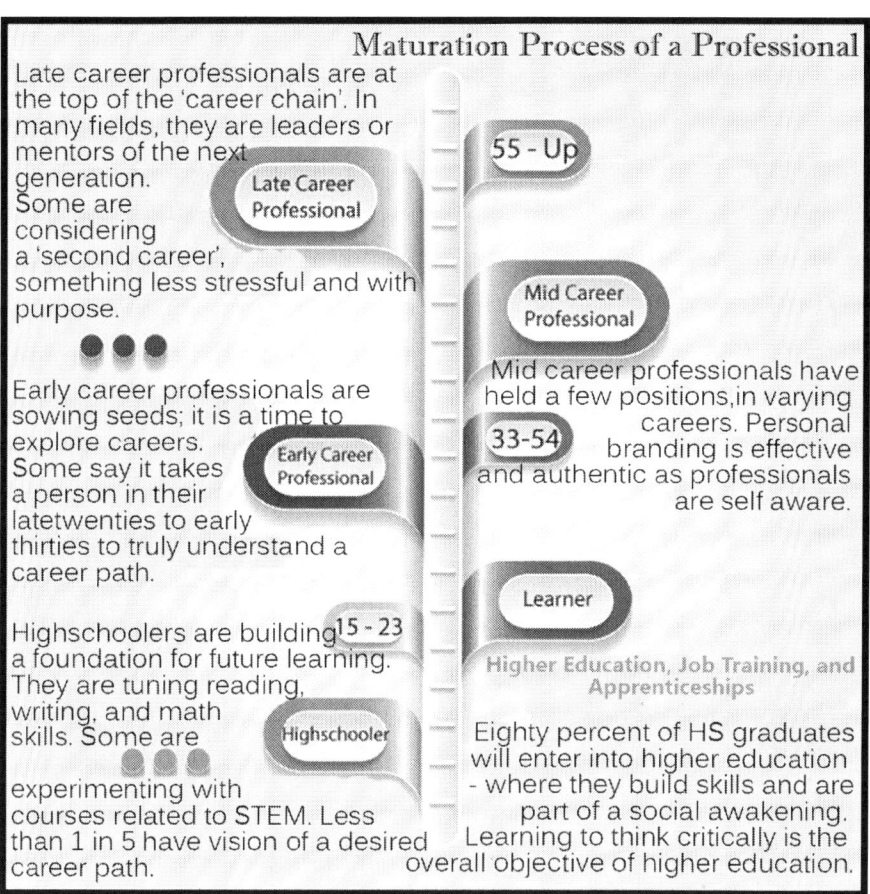

Maturation Process of a Professional

Late career professionals are at the top of the 'career chain'. In many fields, they are leaders or mentors of the next generation. Some are considering a 'second career', something less stressful and with purpose.

Late Career Professional — 55 - Up

Early career professionals are sowing seeds; it is a time to explore careers. Some say it takes a person in their late twenties to early thirties to truly understand a career path.

Early Career Professional — 33-54

Mid career professionals have held a few positions, in varying careers. Personal branding is effective and authentic as professionals are self aware.

Highschoolers are building a foundation for future learning. They are tuning reading, writing, and math skills. Some are experimenting with courses related to STEM. Less than 1 in 5 have vision of a desired career path.

Highschooler — 15 - 23

Learner — Higher Education, Job Training, and Apprenticeships

Eighty percent of HS graduates will enter into higher education - where they build skills and are part of a social awakening. Learning to think critically is the overall objective of higher education.

Personal Branding Challenges

There are parts of personal branding that might seem enjoyable such as becoming self-aware, developing a vision, continual learning and working towards mastery, and making solid connections. However, there are also parts of it that might seem arduous and mechanical. And many of us cringe when told to self-promote and sell ourselves as a brand. Online personal branding is a difficult undertaking for a number of reasons.

Much of the content and communications we publish online becomes part of a permanent record. It is very difficult to get rid of unwanted content from appearing and be accessed online. Like the way Scott Monty of Ford Motor Co. sums up how content can linger on the internet, he says: "Remember: Whatever happens in Vegas... stays on Google" (Glaser, 2009). A recent example is the legal hurdles Europe is going through to get Google to introduce a 'right to be forgotten'. The issue hinges on whether a web service should assist in removing unwanted, dated content from the public domain so a person can recapture his or her identity. You have to make a careful decision when publishing content, while keeping an eye on what other people publish about you.

It is difficult managing personal and professional content, which is something I talked about earlier in the book. When using certain web services, we just want to be ourselves and not worry about the implications of things be taken out of context. Sometimes we want to be funny, challenge the status quo, or be clever. In a way, we want to have multiple identities as we reach out to different channels or as one study put it: "the freedom to explore multiple selves" (Labrecque, Markos, & Milne, 2011). But this is hard to do, and you must always consider how publishing personal content and messages reflect on your personal brand. For example, let's say you watch a music video on YouTube and decide to leave a comment. To do so, you must sign in with your Google account and your profile appears in the comments section below the video. All of a sudden, people make impressions about you based on the type of music you listen to privately.

No matter how we try to erect barriers to protect our privacy, in many cases, we cannot protect our anonymity or the how information is disseminated (Richter, 2013). This requires us to monitor what is out in the public domain about us and how it affects our personal brand, whether it is something we publish or another party publishes. Online personal branding requires being vigilant in protecting your reputation.

Online personal branding mistakes are difficult, sometimes impossible to recover from. As you make more connections in social media and publish content, everything you produce is shared with your audience. If you over generalize or make an out of character remark, your audience can turn on you. The problem is you usually do not get a third or fourth chance to redeem yourself, so a lost connection is tough to win back. Dangling connections are dangerous because you have little assurance how they will back your reputation when the time comes for them to. Also because making connections online is so easy to do, you can tap-out a target audience fairly quickly.

Trying to control perceptions is subjective, which requires constant monitoring and soliciting feedback from a target audience; you cannot know how others perceive you without them telling you in some way. Do not take this for granted; you cannot read other persons' minds. Make self-knowledge and -awareness a priority.

Online personal branding is a requirement, so you are forced to do something about it regardless if it is something you want to do or even like doing; as one study put it: "branding is inevitable when participating in an online environment" (Labrecque, Markos, & Milne, 2011). People are making impressions of you based on what they find out about you online. It is in your best interest to do what you can to control these impressions – corral your digital footprint into a cohesive personal brand. Moreover, if you are seeking employment, the majority of employment evaluations are going to be based a collection of your social media profiles and (hopefully) a personal website – effectively replacing the standard resume.

As discussed earlier, there can be conflicts between your online personal brand and an employer's company brand. On occasion, you might have to acquiesce to the expectations of your employer.

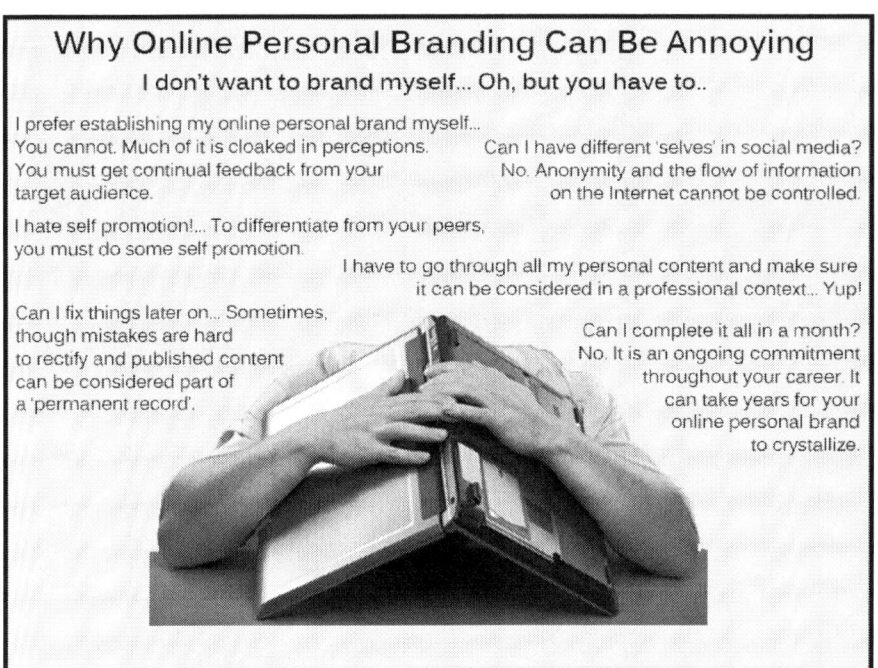

An online personal brand is something you commit to in the long term. It can take years to effectively establish it, so you have to be patient. Do not over extend your presence in social media by rushing to make connections, but rather wait until you have established your identity. Moreover, if you make a major career change, rebranding is another big investment in time and attention.

Conclusion

After reading this book, you are now equipped with a functional model for establishing your online personal brand. I have broken down the nebulous concept of personal branding into three elements: skill set, aura, and identity. There are definitions of each of these elements and where they overlap. Your takeaway is an approach to develop your own online personal brand.

I have also discussed how and why you should project your online personal brand and employ a bottom-up approach whenever possible. There are so many networks and social-media applications available, it is enticing to become enamored with the network effect and neglect to build a strong identity. Yet the connections you make and the content you publish reflects your personal brand.

You want to employ motivational fit to correctly influence your target audience. If your audience is looking for a gain, then provide them with promotion content. If your audience is looking to avoid a loss, then provide them with prevention content. When most people hear the term personal branding, they instantaneously think of self-promotion. But for many professions, there is as much or more prevention required to maximize influence to a target market.

A personal website should be the centerpiece of a personal brand for a few reasons. First and foremost, you own a domain name and all of the content of a personal website. It establishes your identity. Moreover, it is something that stays with you as you navigate through your career. A personal website has an interface to present skills and credentials in many different ways. A powerful way to present skills is through demonstration, and this is possible by using the various forms of media available on a personal website. To infuse your style and flair, a personal website is superior to all other online platforms because it is free-form. You can choose a style, layout, and aesthetics that fit who you are—your aura. Finally, it is something that changes through time.

Being human is a valuable characteristic and an important element of your online personal brand. The simple fact is that machines, computers, and robots are and will continue to displace workers. Any procedure that can be automated may be targeted. Even professions that seem protected are open game. For example, robots can now perform the procedure of an anesthesiologist at a tiny margin of the cost. This means you have to proactively differentiate social skills and find ways to communicate your emotional value through online mediums. In *Average Is Over*, Tyler Cowen sums it up: "Personal qualities of character, such as self-motivation and conscientiousness, will reap a lot of gains in the new world to come" (Cowen, 2013, p. 250).

Whether you have heard about it or not, personal branding has become a requirement for all professions. Experts say that since you have a digital footprint, you already have a personal brand. Interested parties, such as recruiters and potential employers, can find you in a Google search and form an impression about you based on what they find. It is up to you to manage this impression so that it represents you in a favorable way.

There are interesting implications for the millennial generation. They are considered digital natives and already have a huge personal presence in social media. If you are part of this generation, you are going to have to figure out the best way to transition from being a college student to a professional. You will have to decide how to separate your personal and professional content, manage your personal brand within an employer's company brand, and differentiate your personal brand in an increasingly connected world.

I like talking about an online personal brand because I think everyone should spend time building one. It forces you to self-reflect and concentrate on building you, a maturation process that will not only make you successful but also happy and fulfilled. I cannot think of how many people say they wish they had taken a different career path and want to make a change but financial and family obligations make it prohibitive. As you develop an online personal brand, you are compelled to think about what drives you and how you project it to a target audience. Hopefully this process helps you develop a deeper understanding of your skills, values, and passions when making big career decisions, including choosing what degree to pursue, where to live, and what jobs to take early in your career.

Your personal brand is a long-term commitment. It is something you are constantly building and trying to improve. Moreover, it is a characterization of you. In a Forbes article, Glen Llopis says: "Every day, every week, and every month – you must be mindful about how your personal brand as a leader can elevate your relevancy, impact, and influence" (Llopis, 2014). (I believe his assertion is relevant whether or not you consider yourself a leader.)

As you navigate through a career, you may have to take a job for a paycheck to support your family, although, you should always have an eye on the prize: an authentic, personal brand. Partly because of transparency and partly because of connectedness, there has been a convergence between personal and professional values. So if you do not believe in your employer's mission, a coworker takes credit for your work, or you do not feel a sense of fulfillment in your current role, then you should be ready to make a career move (Fuscaldo, 2014). All of these situations have a negative impact on your personal brand.

I find many similarities between a personal brand and what Ken Robinson calls one's element. Perhaps a personal brand is more of an outward expression and an element is more of an inward expression, otherwise the concepts have many similar connotations. In *Finding your Element*, he says, "You not only have to love what you do, you should also enjoy the culture and the tribes that go with it" (Robinson, 2013, p. 191). I think this encapsulates the humanness and connectedness required in the new economy. There is little separation between professional and personal expectations.

There are few barriers with online personal branding. It is inexpensive. Most social-media services are free. You can build profiles and connect with others easily. A personal website has a small monthly fee but is relatively inexpensive. I suggest paying for a personal website, because you are paying for ownership. You own a domain name and all of the content published on it. A provider of a free service typically finds ways to recoup expenses by putting unwanted ads on your website, using your content for marketing purposes, or sharing your information with third-party organizations. This is why I suggest paying for a personal website, exactly as a company pays for its website. It also can be accomplished by incrementally making additions throughout your career. There is no rush to project your online personal brand in one sitting.

Once you have defined and have some success establishing your personal brand, you become wise and live by it. One branding expert says: "consider developing your brand as a strategic platform that serves as your own personal GPS" (Yohn, 2014).

In the appendices, I have provided some tables to help you conceptualize your personal brand. Use them to think about how the key elements of online personal branding work with you, and understand how you are currently represented online collectively.

Appendix A: Diagrams

Online Personal Brand

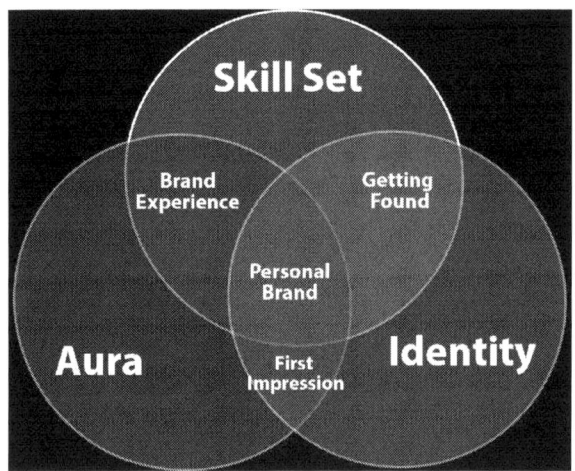

Think about your online personal brand according to the three elements: skill set, aura, and identity. What are your skills? What are your values, personality traits, and charisma? Whom are you connecting with and whom do you want to make connections with? Think about the intersections: brand experience, first impressions, and getting found. Are you authentic? Are you leaving a lasting impression after a fifteen-second viewing of your personal website? Can your target audience find you on LinkedIn, Facebook, and Google? Now think about defining your online personal brand collectively. What is your value proposition in four hundred words? Who is your target audience? Do you have vision and insight regarding where you want to be in ten years?

Projecting Your Brand

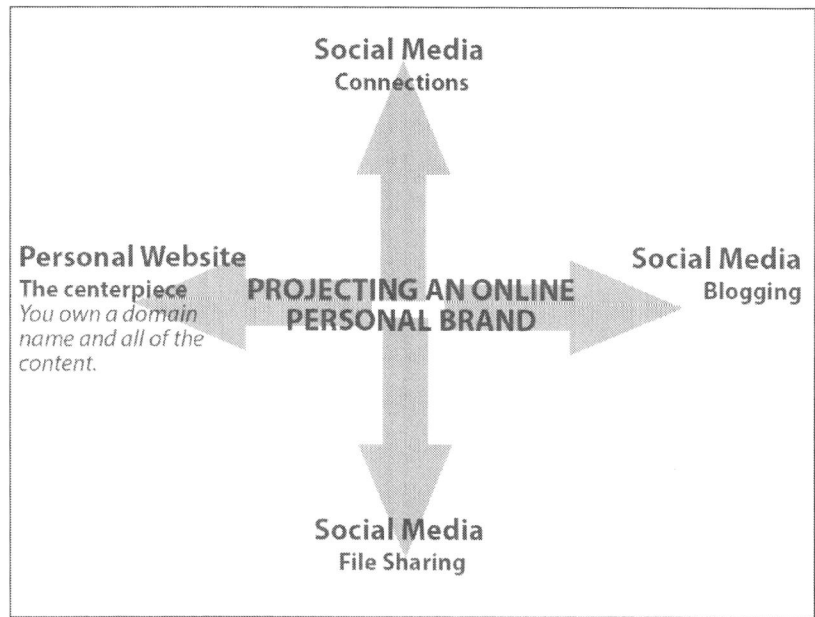

Fill in all the different tools you use to effectively project your brand. Reflect on how you represent *you* in each of the different platforms. Ask yourself: Is the personal brand I am projecting uniform? Should I use other tools to project my personal brand?

Appendix B: Personal Branding Books

Me 2.0: Build a Powerful Brand to Achieve Career Success, **by Dan Schawbel.** The book is an excellent resource for understanding how personal branding can be done in much the same way companies do branding: developing a marketing plan. Some may question whether all professionals can employ some of the tactics. Nevertheless, this is a groundbreaking book regarding personal branding and how it is transforming the requirements of a modern-day professional.

Promote Yourself: The New Rules for Career Success, **by Dan Schawbel.** Schawbel picks up from where he left of in *Me 2.0*. In this book, there is great advice for all professionals to gain influence and success. Some of the themes of the book include discussion of soft, hard, and online skills; cross-generational communication; "intra-preneurship" and entrepreneurship; and the proper use of self-promotion.

Branding Pays: The Five-Step System to Reinvent Your Personal Brand, **by Karen Kang.** Karen Kang provides an elaborate yet effective way to create your personal brand. Moreover, she provides a few examples to illustrate each method. The examples really clarify what she suggests in developing a personal branding strategy.

Social Networking for Career Success: Using Online Tools to Create a Personal Brand, **by Miriam Salpeter.** I look at this book as a resource for applying social media to establish your personal brand. In addition, Ms. Salpeter discusses many of the key elements in online personal branding. I find myself thumbing through the pages to figure out ways to use related online resources.

Reinventing You: Define Your Brand, Imagine Your Future, **by Dorie Clark** This book has some useful new ideas for personal branding. I really like her discussion on using focus groups to understand perceptions. It is focused on professionals transitioning in their careers (as the title of the book suggests).

Career Distinction: Stand Out by Building Your Brand, **by William Arruda and Kirsten Dixson** This book contains a thorough discussion and ample advice related to building a personal brand. It includes many useful links to resources on conceptualizing your personal brand. I think it is useful for all professionals at various stages in their careers.

You Branding: Reinventing Your Personal Identity as a Successful Brand, **by Mark Cijo** This is a recently published (2014) book about personal branding. I appreciate how Mark Cijo talks about projecting a brand – an important concept in online personal branding. (It is something I designate a chapter about in my book.) He also shares good strategies for connecting to an audience on an emotional level.

Authentic Personal Branding, by Herbert K. Rampersad. The author is meticulous in his approach to developing an 'authentic personal brand'. A major theme of the book is a need for self-knowledge: self-awareness and self-regulation. His discussion regarding the alignment of a personal and company brand (something I also discuss) is increasingly relevant as personal branding becomes a requirement for most professionals.

The Brand Called You, By Peter Montoya. This book has lots of great personal branding advice, especially for small business owners or free agents. The author's discussion is often customer centric.

The 10Ks of Personal Branding, By Kaplan Mobray. This book covers many of the major themes of personal branding. It is written as a workbook as the author poses many questions to get you thinking. I like that it is written to a wide audience of professionals.

Appendix C: Millennial Branding Survey

Here are two more charts from the Millennial Survey on personal branding, along with detailed information about the sample used in the survey.

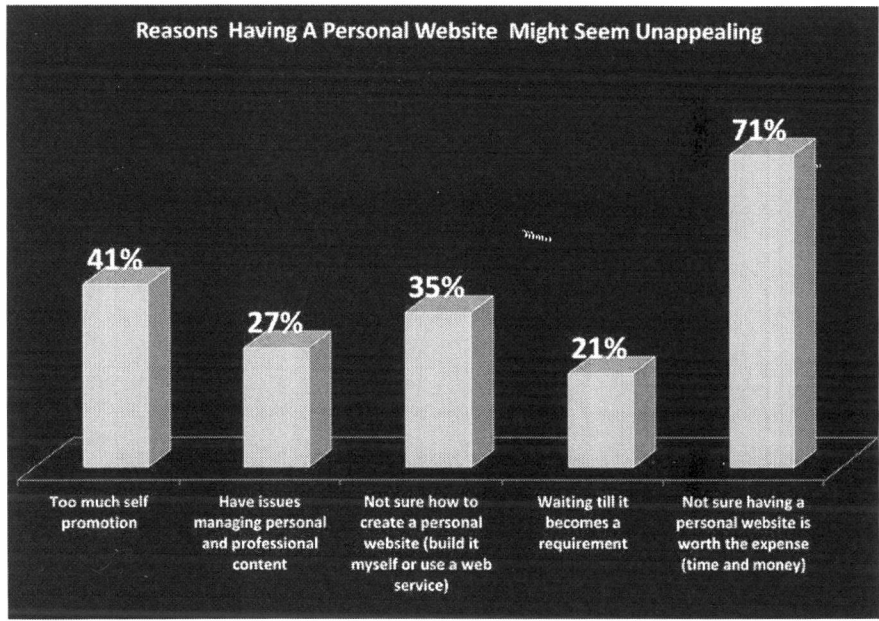

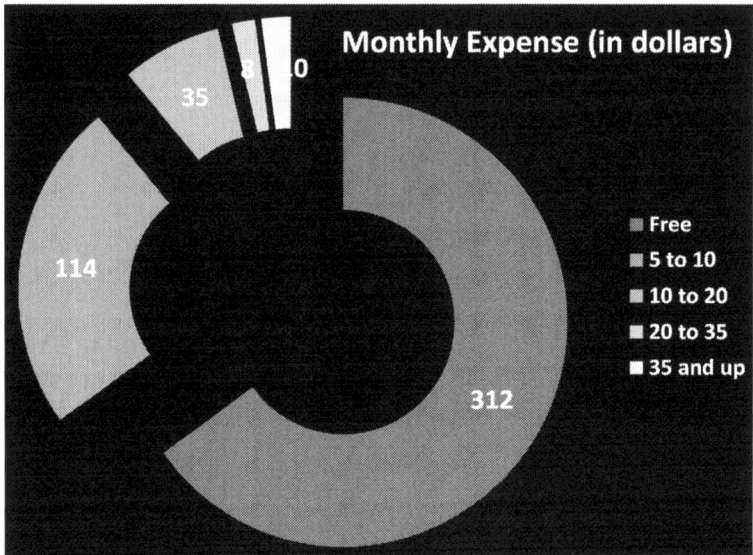

This survey was disseminated using SurveyMonkey, a popular web service. It was sent randomly to over five hundred persons between the ages of eighteen and thirty-three (the demarcation for the millennial generation). The sample size included 479 respondents.

Here is information about the respondents of the survey:
- Gender: 46 percent male and 54 percent female
- Age: 77 percent between eighteen and twenty-nine and 23 percent between thirty and forty-four
- Declared career stage: 49 percent early career, 35 percent college students, 12 percent mid-career, 3 percent high school, and 0.4 percent late career
- Education: 36 percent associate or bachelor degree, 34 percent some college, 21 percent graduate degree, 9 percent high-school degree, and 1 percent less than high-school degree
- Location: 20 percent South Atlantic, 17 percent East-North Central, 14 percent Middle Atlantic, 12 percent Pacific, 11 percent West-North Central, 8 percent West-South Central, 8 percent New England, 5 percent Mountain, and 3 percent East-South Central

Appendix D: Personal Branding Tips

There are so many experts with tips on developing a personal brand. I wanted to make a list of some of my tips:

- ✓ **Create and own a personal website.** This is the single most important aspect of your personal brand. It is something you want to maintain throughout your career. It acts as the centerpiece of your online personal brand. Make sure you own it.
- ✓ **Purchase a domain name.** This is your PO Box on the internet. Make sure it points to your personal website, and using sub-domains, you may use it to point to other elements of your personal brand.
- ✓ **Build and validate a skill set. Work towards mastery with top skills.** The new requirement is committing to lifelong learning. Think of ways to continually build your skill set. Mastery of a few skills reflects strongly on your personal brand.
- ✓ **Control your SERP, so it is a positive reflection you.** People are going to search on your name and content you publish. There are effective ways to manage the results. There are ways get positive links to rank higher, and less flattering links lower.
- ✓ **First establish a professional identity, then project it onto networks.** It is easy and free to join most social media networks. The problem is these networks must advocate the growth of their network, so they cannot also advocate the identity aspect of their service. Do not become enamored by the network effect, make sure your profile is a positive reflection on you.
- ✓ **Identify your target audience. Find ways to reach it – be 'that guy'.** An effective personal brand targets a particular audience. You cannot reach everyone or take a 'pie in the sky' effort with a personal brand. There are

simply too many people in the world. It is also not all about you.
- ✓ **Consistently get feedback from your target audience.** Use focus groups, interviews, surveys, an open door policy, and whatever other means you can to understand how others perceive your personal brand. A heightened awareness gives you an advantage and helps you differentiate.
- ✓ **Pull recruiters and employers to you. Passively seek employment.** You are going to have many job and career changes in your professional career. Make your personal brand accessible to recruiters, so you are always available for a better opportunity.
- ✓ **Show vision. Have short and long term goals.** Professionals with vision standout from the rest. Become more self-aware and set realistic goals.
- ✓ **Deliver visually appealing content.** It is possible to create and publish various forms of media – graphics, video, and slideshows. Make sure you use these forms of media. A striking picture gets etched in the mind of the viewer.
- ✓ **Define and deliver a slogan.** No different from the way companies create a slogan and operationalize on it, do the same with your personal brand. Your slogan should be personal, memorable, and visual.
- ✓ **Make a human to human connection** (Kramer, 2014). Since you can connect with an audience on a personal level, you are expected to do so. Add a personal dimension to your online personal brand. Put your personality, values, and interests on display.
- ✓ **Understand how you want to be perceived by others. Discover how you are actually perceived by others.** Much of your emotional value – your aura – is based on perceptions. Find ways, like focus groups, to truly understand what others think of you.

- ✓ **Apply 'motivational fit'.** Think about what your audience wants to know about you, whether they are looking for a gain or want to prevent a loss. Deliver promotion and/or prevention content based on their preferences (Halerson & Higgins, 2013).
- ✓ **Be authentic and true to yourself.** With your personal brand, you want to effectively tie together all the elements. Make sure your lines do not get crossed. Be consistent.
- ✓ **Tie elements of your personal life into your personal brand.** You can usually find your dominate strengths and attributes on display in your hobbies and personal experiences.
- ✓ **Behaviors and attitudes reflect on your personal brand.** Make sure your actions and responses are in synch with what you say. Communicate your personal brand in all facets of your life.
- ✓ **Make a powerful first impression.** Most of your connections will make a 'knee-jerk' first impression of you. Find ways to make a positive first impression stick.
- ✓ **Focus on your core competencies, values, and passions.** You want to deliver a strong, focused personal brand. So do not dilute its potency by over committing, trying to reach everybody, or trying to be a jack of all trades.
- ✓ **Consider benchmarking.** It is likely there are already well established personal brands similar to what you are trying to accomplish with yours. Consider following them in social media and seeing what they are doing on their personal websites. Evaluate what they do successfully and not so successfully (Celeste, 2014).
- ✓ **Create recognizable pattern and sequences.** String together your educational, employment, and other

experiences together to define your uniqueness and value (Mobray, 2009).

Appendix E: Glossary of Terms

Model: Aura + Skill Set + Identity = Online Personal Brand

Aura – is your personality, value, interests, and charisma. With an online personal brand, it represents your emotional value. It can be challenging to control because it is based on perceptions.

Skill Set – is the combination of skills you have acquired from your education, employment, and other experiences. A skill is an attribute required to complete a task. With an online personal brand, it represents your functional or rational value. There are precise ways to establish credibility with a skill set: references, certifications, and work samples.

Identity – is how you are represented on networks: the connections you make, content or intellectual property ("IP") you publish, and networks you join. With online personal branding, it is a matter of establishing an identity and then projecting it onto networks. You want to own your identity: domain name, personal website, and valuable intellectual property.

Brand Experience – is the merging of your functional and emotional value. For an effective online personal brand, this requires linking your skill set and aura so you are consistent and authentic.

Getting Found – is how you make yourself accessible to a target audient by presenting your skill set. With online personal branding, it represents the intersection of a skill set and identity. By publishing a skill set in various networks (LinkedIn, Monster.com, etc.), you provide recruiters, clients, and associates with key terms to search and find you.

First Impression – is the impact you leave on someone visiting your personal website and/or social media profiles before they learn about your functional capabilities. Typically it is a quick, knee-jerk reaction. With online personal branding, it represents the intersection of an aura and identity.

Concepts

Be 'That Guy' – is a term used to describe how you fit professionally within your network. It describes your primary function (like a job title): 'web designer', 'accountant', 'IP lawyer', etc.

Brand Ambassadors – people from your professional network who speak highly and spread the word regarding your personal brand (Mobray, 2009).

Brand Image – information posted by the focal person, information posted by others, and the marketplace reaction to the presented information (Labrecque, Markos, & Milne, 2011).

Brand Positioning – is how you actively communicate to a target audience.

Digital Brand Audits – is about having a third-party evaluate the effectiveness of your online personal brand. You want to understand whether you are being perceived in a similar way that you want to be perceived.

Elevator Pitch – a short statement (under 300 words) that captures the essence of your personal brand. You want to summarize your strengths, differentiate, and provide a value proposition.

Impression Management – managing the way others perceive you, a core strategy of personal branding (Mobray, 2009).

Motivational Fit – is about gaining influence by matching what people want and how they go about getting it — the way they reach their goals. Some professions will demand more promotion content, while other professions will demand prevention content (Halerson & Higgins, 2013, p. 152).

Slogan – is one to three words that describes what you have to offer in an emotional way. It is not much different than the way companies use slogans to promote their brands.

Target Audience – who you are trying to reach with your employers, partners, associates, and clients. Targeting is critical because you cannot effectively reach everyone with a personal brand. Moreover, personal branding is not all about you.

Notes

Angone, P. (2013). *101 Secrets For Your Twenties.* Chicago: Moody Publishers.

Arruda, W., & Dib, D. (2013). *Ditch Dare Do.* New York: TradeMark Press.

Aruda, W. (2014, June 10th). Why LinkedIn Is The Only Personal Branding Resource You Need. *Forbes*. Retrieved from http://www.forbes.com/sites/williamarruda/2014/06/10/why-linkedin-is-the-only-personal-branding-resource-you-need/

Aruda, W., & Dixson, K. (2007). *Career Distinction: Stand Out By Building Your Brand.* Hoboken: Wiley & Sons.

Arum, R., & Roksa, J. (2011). *Academically Adrift: Limited Learning on College Campuses.* Chicago: University of Chicago Press.

Bianchi, J. (2014, June 17th). Do Job Candidates With Personal Websites Have an Edge. *Forbes*. Retrieved from http://www.forbes.com/sites/learnvest/2014/06/17/do-job-candidates-with-personal-websites-have-an-edge/

Bok, D. (2013). *Higher Education in America.* Princeton: Princeton Univerisity Press.

Bowen, W. (2013). *Higher Education in the Digital Age.* Princeton: Princeton University Press.

Bradberry, T., & Greaves, J. (2009). *Emotional Intelligence 2.0.* San Diego: Talent Smart.

Bronson, P., & Merryman, A. (2013). *Top Dog: The Science of Winning and Losing.* New York.

Celeste, J. (2014). *Find Other to Benchmark for Personal Branding Success.* Retrieved June 21st, 2014, from http://www.jillceleste.com/find-others-to-benchmark-for-personal-branding-success/

Christensen, C. (2011). *Disrupting Class: How Disruptive Innovation Will Change the Way the World Learns.* New York: McGraw Hill.

Churchill, S. (2011). *How to Learn Higher Paying Skills.* Self-published.

Cijo, M. (2014). *You Branding: Reinventing Your Personal Identity As A Successful Brand.* Self-published.

Clark, D. (2013, September 17th). Personal Branding for Introverts. *HBR Blog Network*. Retrieved from http://blogs.hbr.org/2013/09/personal-brnading-for-introverts

Clark, D. (2013). *Reinventing You.* Boston: Harvard Business Review Press.

Cowen, T. (2013). *Average is Over: Powering America Beyond The Age of the Great Stagnation.* New York: Penguin.

Crosby, D. (2012). *You're Not That Great.* Tarentum: Word Association.

Dalla-Camina, M. (2014, May 20th). 5 Keys to Building Your Personal Brand. *Huffington Post*.

Demarais, A., & White, V. (2005). *First Impressions: What You Don't Know About How Others See You.* Bantam Books.

Ellin, A. (2014, June 6th). For Some Retirees, a Second Act Is Easier Than Expected. *The New York Times*. Retrieved from http://www.nytimes.com/2014/06/07/your-money/for-retirees-a-second-career.html

Farren, C. (2014, May). Help New Hire Succeed: Beat the Statistics. Retrieved from http://www.thewynhurstgroup.com/press/ArticleMay07_HelpNewHires.pdf

Frischmann, R. (2012, December 18th). *Scribd.* Retrieved from Push Pull Approach: http://www.scribd.com/doc/117302960/Push-Pull-Approach

Frischmann, R. (2013). *A Skills-Based Approach to Developing a Career.* Trafford.

Fuscaldo, D. (2014, April 21st). 6 Ways Your Job is Losing You Future Earnings. Retrieved from http://www.glassdoor.com/blog/6-ways-job-losing-future-earnings/

Gardner, J. (2013, October 23rd). *Lifehacker.* Retrieved June 25th, 2014, from The "Personal Brand" Myth: http://lifehacker.com/the-personal-brand-myth-1450843371

Glaser, M. (2009, July 16th). *Personal Branding Becomes a Necessity in Digital Age.* Retrieved June 25th, 2014, from PBS: http://www.pbs.org/mediashift/2009/07/personal-branding-becomes-a-necessity-in-digital-age197/

Godin, S. (2010). *Linchpin: Are You Indispensable?* New York: Penguin.

Godin, S. (2012). *The Icarus Deception.* New York: Penguin.

Halerson, H. G., & Higgins, E. T. (2013). *Focus: User Different Ways of Seeing the World for Success and Influence.* New York: Penguin.

Halzack, S. (2013, November 22nd). At Advisory Board, Pro Bono Work Is Central in Attracting, Retaining, and Training Millennials. *The Washington Post.*

Hardy, Q. (2014, April 4th). Writing in a Nonstop World. *NY Times.* Retrieved from http://bits.blogs.nytimes.com/2014/04/26/writing-in-a-nonstop-world/

Hardy, Q. (2014, June 11th). Your Personality Type, Defined by the Internet. *The New York Times.* Retrieved from http://bits.blogs.nytimes.com/2014/06/11/your-personality-type-defined-by-the-internet/

Kang, K. (2013). *Branding Pays The Five-Step System to Reinvent Your Personal Brand.* Palo Alto: Branding Pays LLC.

Kramer, B. (2014). *Human to Human: H2H.* PureMatter.

Labrecque, L. I., Markos, E., & Milne, G. R. (2011). Online Personal Branding: Processes, Challenges, and Implications. *Journal of Interactive Marketing*, pp. 37-50. Retrieved from http://www.laurenlabrecque.com/wp-content/uploads/2012/12/2011_JIM.pdf

Lederman, G. (2007). *Achieve Brand Integrity.* Rochester: B@W Press.

Lee, K. (2014, June 26th). The Art of Self-Promotion on Social Media. *Fast Company*. Retrieved from http://www.fastcompany.com/3032287/hit-the-ground-running/the-art-of-self-promotion-on-social-media

Lewis, S. (2014). *The Rise: Creativity, The Gift of Failure, and the Search for Mastery.* New York: Simon & Schuster.

Llopis, G. (2014, June 11th). Personal Branding Represents Your Distinction And Responsibility As A Leader. *Forbes*. Retrieved from http://www.forbes.com/sites/glennllopis/2014/06/11/personal-branding-represents-your-distinction-and-responsibility-as-a-leader

Marrs, M. (2012, February 14th). The First Step to Building Your Personal Brand. *Forbes*. Retrieved from http://www.forbes.com/sites/dailymuse/2012/02/14/the-first-step-to-building-your-personal-brand

Metz, C. (2013, March). Donglegate Controversy Yields Only One Winner: GitHub. *Wired*.

Mobray, K. (2009). *The 10Ks of Personal Branding.* New York: iUniverse, Inc.

Montoya, P. (2009). *The Brand Called You.* McGraw Hill.

Mozilla. (n.d.). Open Badges Working Papers. Retrieved from http://wiki/mozilla.org/File: OpenBadges-Working-Paper_012312.pdf

National Center for Education Statistics. (n.d.). Retrieved June 5th, 2014, from http://nces.ed.gov/fastfacts/display.asp?id=40

Newport, C. (2012). *So Good They Cannot Ignore You: Why Skills Trump Passion in the Quest for Work You Love.* New York: Hachett.

Pappers, A. (2014, April 22nd). 5 Tips for Improving Your Personal Brand. *Guardian*.

Peters, T. (1997). The Brand Called You. *Fast Company*.

Porter, C. (2013, September 30th). Millennials Face Uphill Climb. *WSJ*.

Protalinksi, E. (2014, April 29th). Twitter passes 255m monthly active users, 198m mobile users, and sees 80% of advertising revenue from mobile. *TheNextWeb*. Retrieved from http://thenextweb.com/twitter/2014/04/29/twitter-passes-255m-monthly-active-users-198m-mobile-users-sees-80-advertising-revenue-mobile/

Rampersad, H. K. (2009). *Authentic Personal Branding.* Charlotte: Information Age Publishing.

Rega, P. (2013). *12 Steps to Freedom.* Self-published.

Richter, S. (2013, August 28th). *A Dozen Ways to Build Your Personal Brand In an Online World.* Retrieved June 6th, 2014, from Socialmedia Today:

http://socialmediatoday.com/samrichter/1700011/ways-build-personal-brand-online-world

Ries, L. (2012). *Visual Hammer.* Self-published.

Robinson, K. (2013). *Finding Your Element: How to Discover Your Talents and Passions and Transform Your Life.* New York: Penguin.

Rosen, N. (2012, December). What's the Cash Value of Your Brand. *Business Insider.* Retrieved from http://www.businessinsider.com/whats-the-cash-value-of-your-brand-2012-12

Salpeter, M. (2011). *Social Networking for Career Success.* New York: Learning Express.

Salpeter, M., & Morgan, H. (2013). *Social Networking for Business Success.* New York: Learning Express.

Sandholm, D. (2014, May 28th). *CNBC.* Retrieved June 7th, 2014, from LinkedIn CEO reveals growth strategy: http://www.cnbc.com/id/101710272

Schawbel, D. (2009). *Me 2.0: Build a Powerful Brand to Acheive Career Success.* New York: Kaplan Publishing.

Schawbel, D. (2013). *Promote Yourself: The New Rules For Career Success.* New York: St. Martin's Press.

Selingo, J. J. (2013). *College (Un) Bound: The Future of Higher Education and What it Means for Students.* Self-published.

Shellenbarger, S. (2014, April 29th). When it Comes to Work, Can You Care Too Much? *WSJ.*

Smith, E., & Aaker, J. (2013, November 30th). Millennial Searchers. *The New York Times.*

Sterlacci, P. (2013). Personal Brands Are Like a Sweet Onion. *Personal Branding Blog*. Retrieved from http://www.personalbrandingblog.com/personal-brands-are-like-a-sweet-onion

Taylor, P. (2014). *The Next America: Boomers, Millennials, and the Looming Generational Showdown.* Perseus.

Troung, A. (2014, June 4th). LinkedIn Tweaks User Profile Design, Now Looks More Like Facebook. *Fast Company*. Retrieved from http://www.fastcompany.com/3031470/most-innovative-companies/linkedin-tweaks-users-profile-designs-now-looks-more-like-facebook

Tulathimutte, T. (2013, September 4th). You Are What You Tweet. *The New Yorker*. Retrieved from http://www.newyorker.com/online/blogs/currency/2013/09/personal-branding-you-are-what-you-tweet.html

Vaughan, P. (2012, August 21st). *Visual Content Trumps Text in Driving Social Media Engagement [INFOGRAPHIC]*. Retrieved June 11th, 2014, from HubSpot : http://blog.hubspot.com/blog/tabid/6307/bid/33513/Visual-Content-Trumps-Text-in-Driving-Social-Media-Engagement-INFOGRAPHIC.aspx#ixzz25YEUnjwp

Wagner, K. (2014, April 23rd). Facebook Passes 1 Billion Monthly Mobile Users. *Mashable*. Retrieved from http://mashable.com/2014/04/23/facebook-1-billion-mobile-users/

Wang, N. (2012). *The Resume is Dead.* Self-published.

Weber, J. (2014, May 11th). Should Companies Monitor Their Employees' Social Media. *WSJ*.

Wikipedia. (n.d.). Retrieved June 12th, 2014, from
http://en.wikipedia.org/wiki/Reed's_law

Yohn, D. (2014, June 5th). *How Strong Is Your Personal Brand?* Retrieved June 8th, 2014, from Personal Branding Blog: http://www.personalbrandingblog.com/how-strong-is-your-personal-brand

Made in the USA
Lexington, KY
22 August 2014